The Last Days

What's Ahead for the Body of Christ, the Apostate Church, and the World ...

Bill Rudge

LIVING TRUTH PUBLISHERS

A Division of Bill Rudge Ministries, Inc.
Hermitage, Pennsylvania

The Last Days

Library of Congress Catalog Card Number: 98-65516
ISBN 1-889809-02-0

Copyright © 1999 by Bill Rudge

Published by Living Truth Publishers
A Division of Bill Rudge Ministries, Inc.
Hermitage, Pennsylvania

Cover Design and Illustration by David A. Sabella

Printed in the United States of America

Contents

Seven Mountain Peaks of Bible Prophecy

Times are rapidly changing. We are in the birth pains of a coming new world. Before God's new world is ushered in, there will arise a counterfeit new world order causing many changes in society, technology, morality, nature, politics, and religion. To be uninformed of the implications of what is ahead could mean disastrous consequences.

Where is all this change taking us? What does it mean? It seems like the world is rapidly approaching some future destiny, but what is it? Are we living in the last days?

After a time of intense Scripture study, prayer and fasting, and seeking the Lord for insight on the last days, I have written what I see in the near future for the body of Christ, the apostate church, and the world. Comparing Matthew 24 with passages from Revelation, I offer the following overview of seven mountain peaks which are rapidly coming into focus regarding last days prophecies:

1) *Deception of the World and the Apostate Church — False Unity Movement, False Peace, and False Signs and Wonders:*

Deception will increase, leading to the advent of the rider on the white horse (Antichrist). An increasing move toward a false unity and peace, which the apostate church will wrongly discern as revival, will occur. There will be an escalation of false signs and wonders combined with bizarre phenomena and behavior that go beyond the Word of God but will be attributed to the Holy Spirit.

Matthew 24:4,5,24,25 —

Jesus answered: "Watch out that no one deceives you. For many will come in My name, claiming, 'I am the Christ,' and will deceive many. For false Christs and false prophets will appear and perform great signs and miracles to deceive even the elect — if that were possible. See, I have told you ahead of time."

Revelation 6:1,2 —

I watched as the Lamb opened the first of the seven seals. Then I heard one of the four living creatures say in a voice like thunder, "Come!" I looked, and there before me was a white horse! Its rider held a bow, and he was given a crown, and he rode out as a conqueror bent on conquest.

The world and the apostate church are being prepared for the deceptive and seductive reign of the Antichrist. We are rapidly heading into a unified global society and the mark of the beast. However, true believers in Christ who are in God's Word and walking in discernment will not be deceived (I Thessalonians 5:1-4).

2) *Beginning of Birth Pains — Signs of the Times Being Fulfilled:*

We are going to see an increase of wars and rumors of wars as the rider on the red horse removes peace from the earth. Earthquakes will also increase and intensify worldwide. Famine will occur in various places across the earth as the rider on the black horse comes forth.

Matthew 24:6-8 —

You will hear of wars and rumors of wars, but see to it that you are not alarmed. Such things must happen, but the end is still to come. Nation will rise against nation, and kingdom against kingdom. There will be famines and earthquakes in various places. All these are the beginning of birth pains.

Revelation 6:3,4 —

When the Lamb opened the second seal, I heard the second living creature say, "Come!" Then another horse came out, a fiery red one. Its rider was given power to take peace from the earth and to make men slay each other. To him was given a large sword.

Revelation 6:5,6 —

When the Lamb opened the third seal, I heard the third living creature say, "Come!" I looked, and there before me was a black horse! Its rider was holding a pair of scales in his hand. Then I heard what sounded like a voice among the four living creatures, saying, "A quart of wheat for a day's wages, and three quarts of barley for a day's wages, and do not damage the oil and the wine!"

Scripture indicates we will also see an increase of abnormal and bizarre weather conditions worldwide, in addition to famine, plagues, pestilence, violence, immorality, and sorcery.

3) *Persecution and Martyrdom of Believers:*

Worldwide persecution of true believers in Christ is quickly spreading. It will reach its consummation with the Antichrist and False Prophet, who will persecute and martyr those who do not worship the Antichrist and his image and do not receive his mark.

When the rider on the pale horse comes forth, resulting in death to a fourth of the earth by sword, famine, plague, and wild beasts, there will be a frenzied martyrdom of true believers in Christ.

Matthew 24:9-13 —

Then you will be handed over to be persecuted and put to death, and you will be hated by all nations because of Me. At that time many will turn away from the faith and will betray and hate each other, and many false prophets will appear and deceive many people. Because of the increase of wickedness, the love of most will grow cold, but he who stands firm to the end will be saved.

Revelation 6:7,8 —

When the Lamb opened the fourth seal, I heard the voice of the fourth living creature say, "Come!" I looked, and there before me was a pale horse! Its rider was named Death, and Hades was following close behind him. They were given power over a fourth of the earth to kill by sword, famine and plague, and by the wild beasts of the earth.

Revelation 6:9-11 —

When He opened the fifth seal, I saw under the altar the souls of those who had been slain because of the Word of God and the testimony they had maintained. They called out in a loud voice, "How long, Sovereign Lord, holy and true, until You judge the inhabitants of the earth and avenge our blood?" Then each of them was given a white robe, and they were told to wait a little longer, until the number of their fellow servants and brothers who were to be killed as they had been was completed.

Revelation 7:9,14 —

After this I looked and there before me was a great multitude that no one could count, from every nation, tribe, people and language, standing before the throne and in front of the Lamb. They were wearing white robes and were holding palm branches in their hands. ... These are they who have come out of the great tribulation; they have washed their robes and made them white in the blood of the Lamb.

Revelation 13:9,10 —

He who has an ear, let him hear. If anyone is to go into captivity, into captivity he will go. If anyone is to be killed with the sword, with the sword he will be killed. This calls for patient endurance and faithfulness on the part of the saints.

4) *Gospel Preached throughout the World during Time of Persecution:*

In the midst of severe persecution and martyrdom, the Gospel will be preached to the whole world through empowered believers such as the 144,000 (Revelation 7:1-17) who will not love their lives so much as to shrink from death. They will overcome through the blood of the Lamb and the word of their testimony.

Matthew 24:14 —

And this Gospel of the kingdom will be preached in the whole world as a testimony to all nations, and then the end will come.

Revelation 14:6,7 —

Then I saw another angel flying in midair, and he had the eternal Gospel to proclaim to those who live on the earth — to every nation, tribe, language and people. He said in a loud voice, "Fear God and give Him glory, because the hour of His judgment has come. Worship Him who made the heavens, the earth, the sea and the springs of water."

The promised revival of Joel 2:28-32 seems to occur during the Tribulation period. According to Peter's words (Acts 2:17-21) the outpouring of the

Holy Spirit on the day of Pentecost was an initial fulfillment or the firstfruits of Joel's prophecy.

The similar description of Joel 2:30,31 with Revelation 6:12-14 strongly indicates that the ultimate prophesied outpouring of God's Spirit and true revival will occur during the Tribulation period and the Millennium. Also consider that the great multitude that no one can number, from every nation, tribe, people, and language standing before the throne who have washed their robes, and made them white in the blood of the Lamb, have come out of the Great Tribulation (Revelation 7:9,14).

5) *Abomination of Desolation:*

When the Antichrist desecrates the Temple in Jerusalem, the Jews will be severely persecuted and would be annihilated (reduced to nonexistence) if the days were not shortened. At the midpoint of the seven-year Tribulation, when the Antichrist claims to be God and demands worship, he will initiate the worst persecution of the Jews in the history of the world.

Matthew 24:15-21 —

So when you see standing in the holy place "the abomination that causes desolation," spoken of through the prophet Daniel — let the reader understand — then let those who are in Judea flee to the mountains. ... For then there will be great distress, unequaled from the beginning of the world until now — and never to be equaled again.

Jeremiah 30:7 —

How awful that day will be! None will be like it. It will be a time of trouble for Jacob, but he will be saved out of it.

Daniel 12:1 —

... There will be a time of distress such as has not happened from the beginning of nations until then ....

6) *God's Judgment and Wrath — Signs in the Heavens:*

God will ultimately intervene by pouring out His judgment and wrath on those who have accepted the mark of the beast.

Cataclysmic signs in the heavens and on earth will increasingly intensify as God's wrath is meted out on a rebellious world. The opening of the sixth and seventh seals will lead to the trumpet and bowl judgments (listed in Revelation chapters 8-16), with the culmination at Armageddon, where the vultures will gather to eat the carcasses of those assembled to fight against the returning Christ.

Matthew 24:29 —

Immediately after the distress of those days "the sun will be darkened, and the moon will not give its light; the stars will fall from the sky, and the heavenly bodies will be shaken."

Luke 21:25,26 —

There will be signs in the sun, moon and stars. On the earth, nations will be in anguish and perplexity at the roaring and tossing of the sea. Men will faint from terror, apprehensive of what is coming on the world, for the heavenly bodies will be shaken.

Revelation 6:12-17 —

I watched as He opened the sixth seal. There was a great earthquake. The sun turned black like sackcloth made of goat hair, the whole moon turned blood red, and the stars in the sky fell to earth, as late figs drop from a fig tree when shaken by a strong wind. The sky receded like a scroll, rolling up, and every mountain and island was removed from its place.

Then the kings of the earth, the princes, the generals, the rich, the mighty, and every slave and every free man hid in caves and among the rocks of the mountains. They called to the mountains and the rocks, "Fall on us and hide us from the face of Him who sits on the throne and from the wrath of the Lamb! For the great day of their wrath has come, and who can stand?"

Revelation 8:1-6 —

When He opened the seventh seal, there was silence in heaven for about half an hour. And I saw the seven angels who stand before God, and to them were given seven trumpets. Another angel, who had a golden censer, came and stood at the altar. He was given much incense to offer, with the prayers of all the saints, on the golden altar before the throne. The smoke of the incense, together with the prayers of the saints, went up before God from the angel's hand. Then the angel took the censer, filled it with fire from the altar, and hurled it on the earth; and there came peals of thunder, rumblings, flashes of lightning and an earthquake. Then the seven angels who had the seven trumpets prepared to sound them.

Revelation 15:1; 16:1 —

I saw in heaven another great and marvelous sign: seven angels with the seven last plagues — last, because with them God's wrath is completed. Then I heard a loud voice from the temple saying to the seven angels, "Go, pour out the seven bowls of God's wrath on the earth."

7) *Sign of the Son of Man — the Second Coming of Christ:*

Jesus Christ returns in great power and glory. The Antichrist and False Prophet are defeated at Armageddon. The Millennium is ushered in as Satan is bound a thousand years. The final rebellion of Gog and Magog at the end of the Millennium is terminated and Satan is thrown into the lake of fire. The Great White

Throne judgment is completed, the New Jerusalem arrives, and eternity commences.

Matthew 24:27-31 —

For as lightning that comes from the east is visible even in the west, so will be the coming of the Son of Man. Wherever there is a carcass, there the vultures will gather. Immediately after the distress of those days "the sun will be darkened, and the moon will not give its light; the stars will fall from the sky, and the heavenly bodies will be shaken." At that time the sign of the Son of Man will appear in the sky, and all the nations of the earth will mourn. They will see the Son of Man coming on the clouds of the sky, with power and great glory. And He will send His angels with a loud trumpet call, and they will gather His elect from the four winds, from one end of the heavens to the other.

Revelation 19:11-16 —

I saw heaven standing open and there before me was a white horse, whose Rider is called Faithful and True. With justice He judges and makes war. His eyes are like blazing fire, and on His head are many crowns. He has a name written on Him that no one knows but He Himself. He is dressed in a robe dipped in blood, and His name is the Word of God.

The armies of heaven were following Him, riding on white horses and dressed in fine linen, white and clean. Out of His mouth comes a sharp sword with which to strike down the nations. "He will rule them with an iron scepter." He treads the winepress of the fury of the wrath of God Almighty. On His robe and on His thigh He has this name written: King of Kings and Lord of Lords.

Revelation 19:17-21 —

And I saw an angel standing in the sun, who cried in a loud voice to all the birds flying in midair, "Come, gather together for the great supper of God, so that you may eat the flesh of kings, generals, and mighty men, of horses and their riders, and the flesh of all people, free and slave, small and great."

Then I saw the beast and the kings of the earth and their armies gathered together to make war against the Rider on the horse and His army. But the beast was captured, and with him the false prophet .... The two of them were thrown alive into the fiery lake of burning sulfur. The rest of them were killed with the sword that came out of the mouth of the Rider on the horse, and all the birds gorged themselves on their flesh.

Consequences of Disobedience

Why will these catastrophic events of Revelation occur? Obviously to fulfill God's plan for the ages. But also, from a practical perspective, we must remember that God promised great blessings for obedience to Him and His Word (Leviticus 26:3-13; Deuteronomy 28:1-14), as well as restoration for those who repented of violating His Word (Leviticus 26:40-45; Isaiah 1:18,19). However, He promised harsh punishment for those who defiantly rebelled and persistently disobeyed. As we read God's strong warning through Moses in Deuteronomy 28 (also consider Leviticus 26:14-39 and Isaiah 1:2-31), keep in mind the consequences of disobedience. Some of these consequences are already being meted out on our country and around the world. They will ultimately fulfill what Revelation and end-time prophecies say is coming upon a rebellious, unrepentant world and the apostate church.

Excerpts of Deuteronomy 28:15-68 reveal how precisely accurate God's Word has proven to be throughout history and how tragically accurate it will one day soon prove to be —

If you do not obey the Lord your God and do

not carefully follow all His commands and decrees I am giving you today, all these curses will come upon you and overtake you: You will be cursed in the city and cursed in the country. ... The fruit of your womb will be cursed, and the crops of your land, and the calves of your herds and the lambs of your flocks.

... The Lord will strike you with wasting disease, with fever and inflammation, with scorching heat and drought, with blight and mildew, which will plague you until you perish. The sky over your head will be bronze, the ground beneath you iron. The Lord will turn the rain of your country into dust and powder; it will come down from the skies until you are destroyed.

The Lord will cause you to be defeated before your enemies. You will come at them from one direction but flee from them in seven, and you will become a thing of horror to all the kingdoms on earth. Your carcasses will be food for all the birds of the air and the beasts of the earth, and there will be no one to frighten them away. The Lord will afflict you with the boils of Egypt and with tumors, festering sores and the itch, from which you cannot be cured. The Lord will afflict you with madness, blindness and confusion of mind. At midday you will grope about like a blind man in the dark. You will be unsuccessful in everything you do; day after day you will be oppressed and robbed, with no one to rescue you.

... Your sons and daughters will be given to another nation, and you will wear out your eyes watching for them day after day, powerless to lift a hand. A people that you do not know will eat what your land and labor produce, and you will have nothing but cruel oppression all your days. The sights you see will drive you mad. The Lord will afflict your knees and legs with painful boils that cannot be cured, spreading from the soles of your feet to the top of your head.

The Lord will drive you and the king you set over you to a nation unknown to you or your fathers. There you will worship other gods, gods of wood and stone. You will become a thing of horror and an object of scorn and ridicule to all the nations where the Lord will drive you.

... The alien who lives among you will rise above you higher and higher, but you will sink lower and lower. He will lend to you, but you will not lend to him. He will be the head, but you will be the tail.

All these curses will come upon you. They will pursue you and overtake you until you are destroyed, because you did not obey the Lord your God and observe the commands and decrees He gave you. They will be a sign and a wonder to you and your descendants forever. Because you did not serve the Lord your God joyfully and gladly in the time of prosperity, therefore in hunger and thirst, in nakedness and dire poverty, you will serve the enemies the Lord sends against you.

... If you do not carefully follow all the words of this Law, which are written in this Book, and do not revere this glorious and awesome Name — the Lord your God — the Lord will send fearful plagues on you and your descendants, harsh and prolonged disasters, and severe and lingering illnesses ....

Daniel knew the reality concerning the fulfillment of God's promise of curse or blessing. He stated in his prayer given while in Babylonian captivity —

Just as it is written in the Law of Moses, all this disaster has come upon us, yet we have not sought the favor of the Lord our God by turning from our sins and giving attention to Your truth (Daniel 9:13).

Judgment Is Coming

The Lord has withheld His hand of ultimate judgment through all the abominations this present world has flaunted in His face — abortion, sexual immorality, sorcery, violence, deceit, injustice, and so on. Nevertheless, His ultimate judgment will come, for even many in the Church have become corrupt and are spiritual prostitutes — involving themselves in beliefs and practices that are an abomination to the Lord.

The Church's loss of fear and respect for the Lord has resulted in rampant sexual immorality, idolatry, and tolerance of sin. The so-called revival and the supposed new moving of the Holy Spirit consisting of phenomena which are occultic and demonic in nature are a stench in God's nostrils. This unrepentant apostate church will grow and prosper and become even stronger — for awhile — but God's judgment will come swiftly and with certainty.

Choose today whether you will follow a false revival or Biblical Christianity — the faith once for all delivered to the saints. Your testimony for the Word of God and the Jesus of the Bible may cost your life, but you will gain eternity and all that God has prepared for those who remain faithful to Him.

Signs of the Times

I believe that you and I are living in the most exciting time in the history of the world. We are about to witness the fulfillment of what the prophets foretold thousands of years ago.

I realize that many of these signs have occasionally occurred throughout history and many people have wrongly concluded that they were the generation to see Christ return. We've had false prophets. We've had wars and rumors of wars. We've had earthquakes. We've had famines and pestilence, but never before in history have we seen such an increase in both intensity and frequency of these and many other indicating factors. No other generation has ever witnessed the simultaneous coming together of so many prophetic events. Our generation has more potential than any other generation to see the actual fulfillment of Revelation.

Although I became a believer in Jesus Christ through a prophetic ministry, I wasn't convinced back in 1971 that we were about to see Christ return any day. I believed that several things needed to occur in the world before we could see the fulfillment of what the Word of God foretold. However, my attitude began to change and intensify in conviction as the years passed. God's Word and Spirit and my research convinced me that we are the generation (Matthew 24:34) and we must prepare for His soon return.

Signs of His First Coming Went Unheeded

Jesus encountered religious leaders who demanded a sign —

> The Pharisees and Sadducees came to Jesus and tested Him by asking Him to show them a sign from heaven. He replied, "When evening comes, you say, 'It will be fair weather, for the sky is red,' and in the morning, 'Today it will be stormy, for the sky is red and overcast.' You know how to interpret the appearance of the sky, but you cannot interpret the signs of the times" (Matthew 16:1-3).

The signs of the times Jesus was referring to were those concerning His first coming. Those Pharisees and Sadducees, who were *experts* in the Old Testament law and prophets, should have known that Jesus Christ was the promised Messiah because of the prophecies in the Hebrew Scriptures He was fulfilling. They did not discern the signs of their times.

What the Pharisees and Sadducees were guilty of then, many are guilty of today. We do not recognize the signs of the times being fulfilled in our very midst that indicate we are on the verge of the Second Coming of Jesus Christ.

Because the Jewish leaders of Christ's day did not recognize the time of His coming and therefore rejected Him as their Messiah, Jesus prophesied in Luke 19:43,44 —

> The days will come upon you when your enemies will build an embankment against you and encircle you and hem you in on every side.

They will dash you to the ground, you and the children within your walls. They will not leave one stone on another, because you did not recognize the time of God's coming to you.

This tragic prophecy was fulfilled in A.D. 70 by the Romans under Titus. How much more the consequences for those today who do not discern and prepare for His Second Coming.

Extreme Perspectives

There are two extreme perspectives many Christians have in regard to the last days and, as a result, are Biblically imbalanced. First, there are those who want to quit their job, sell everything they own, and go sit on some mountain and pray and fast and wait till Christ returns. Second, there are those who get so caught up in the cares of the world that they become indifferent and don't discern the signs of the times.

Instead, we should have a Biblically balanced perspective. We should be alert and prepared as though He is coming today. However, we should also be about the Father's business, working while it is yet day and occupying until He returns.

During the temptation in Genesis 3, Eve added to God's words by stating, "You must not touch it [the tree of the knowledge of good and evil]," while the serpent took away from God's words by saying, "You will not surely die." In light of this, and the fact that God has repeatedly warned not to add to or subtract from His Word — a warning which has usually gone unheeded, He strongly states in Revelation 22:18,19 —

> I warn everyone who hears the words of the prophecy of this book: If anyone adds anything to them, God will add to him the plagues described in this book. And if anyone takes words away from this book of prophecy, God will take away from him his share in the tree of life and in the holy city, which are described in this book.

We must not carelessly speculate or sensationalize God's prophetic Word in order to make it fit with the current headlines, thus adding to it. We also must not water down nor merely spiritualize prophecies that in context and in light of other literally fulfilled prophecies clearly indicate actual fulfillment, lest we be guilty of taking away from God's prophetic Word.

Some have set dates concerning when they believed Christ would return, but it didn't happen. There has been no shortage of incorrect dates forecasting the time of Christ's return. Matthew 24:36,42 says —

No one knows about that day or hour, not even the angels in heaven, nor the Son, but only the Father. Therefore keep watch, because you do not know on what day your Lord will come.

Scripture, however, indicates that we can know the season (Matthew 24:32-34). We can tell that we are that generation by observing the signs of the times.

There are also those who attempt to identify the Antichrist, but they too have been proven inaccurate. I believe Satan gives many people false visions and revelations, leading them to unscriptural and sensationalized conclusions. Calling themselves Christians, they spout off fraudulent and inaccurate claims. The world, seeing the ludicrous nature of these claims, lumps all Christians believing in end-time prophecies together and labels them as mindless fanatics. Consequently, many reject Biblical Christianity and do not recognize the genuine signs recorded in Scripture that are occurring.

Prophecies Are Being Fulfilled

Although prophecies in the Bible are being fulfilled before our very eyes, Satan has the masses brain-washed into believing that Scripture is outdated, full of error, and irrelevant. The world perceives Biblical Christians as dogmatic and divisive troublemakers, and ministers as charlatans. Therefore, considering the claims of Scripture, studying Bible prophecy, or giving one's life to Christ are not even options for many.

So I caution you to keep your views concerning the last days in Biblical balance. As excited as I am about all the prophecies being fulfilled in this generation, we must not sensationalize, distort, exaggerate, or propagate beliefs that are unfounded, lest we hinder the advancement of the Gospel of Jesus Christ.

The terms "last days" and "last hour" refer to the whole church age, beginning with Christ's first coming (Acts 2:17; Hebrews 1:1,2; I John 2:18). I am convinced, however, that we are rapidly accelerating toward the climax and culmination of this "last days" period, and the return of Christ.

Nature is Out of Control

Throughout the world we are seeing record-breaking heat waves and droughts; some of history's fiercest hurricanes, tornados, volcanos, tsunamis, fires, floods, and mudslides; earthquakes in diverse places; pollution of water, land, and air; widespread famine, plague, and pestilence; and an increase of attacks by wild animals. Nature seems out of control and is becoming more and more extreme. It is moving toward what Revelation indicates will occur during the Tribulation period. The increasing frequency and intensity of out-of-control weather conditions and the "shaking of the earth" (Hebrews 12:26-28; Haggai 2:6) testifies that some cataclysmic global event or cosmic upheaval (sun and moon darkened, stars falling from the sky, and every island and mountain being removed from its place — Matthew 24:29; Revelation 6:14) is near.

The book of Revelation describes the ultimate consummation of the seemingly out-of-control weather conditions. If you think some of our recent droughts and hot spells have been rough, look at Revelation 8:7 —

The first angel sounded his trumpet, and there came hail and fire mixed with blood, and it was hurled down upon the earth. A third of the earth was burned up, a third of the trees were burned up, and all the green grass was burned up.

Revelation 16:8,9 says —

The fourth angel poured out his bowl on the sun, and the sun was given power to scorch people with fire. They were seared by the intense heat and they cursed the name of God, who had control over these plagues, but they refused to repent and glorify Him.

Violence

In Noah's day the world was filled with violence: "Now the earth was corrupt in God's sight and was full of violence" (Genesis 6:11). Violence often leads to bloodshed, and according to Numbers 35:33, "bloodshed pollutes the land."

What do we see today? Throughout the world we see terrorism, hijackings, kidnappings, bombings, assassinations, senseless homicides, serial killings, mass murders, gang violence, abortions, robberies, assaults, demonstrations, and riots. We also are hearing of "wars and rumors of wars" (Matthew 24:6) and "nation rising against nation" (Matthew 24:7). The Greek word for nation is *ethnos*, from which we get our English word "ethnic." We see much ethnic conflict in the world today.

In contrast to the prophesied violence, wars and rumors of wars, and nation rising against nation, which "are the beginning of birth pains" (Matthew 24:8), Paul says that they will be speaking of peace and safety.

I Thessalonians 5:1-4 states —

Now, brothers, about times and dates we do not need to write to you, for you know very well that the day of the Lord will come like a thief in the night. While people are saying, "Peace and safety," destruction will come on them suddenly, as labor pains on a pregnant woman, and they will not escape. But you, brothers, are not in darkness so that this day should surprise you like a thief.

Scripture seems confusing at this point. How could it indicate the world would be filled with violence, and then on the other hand reveal that people would be saying "peace and safety"? But in our generation many unclear Scriptural prophecies are beginning to come into focus. We are seeing the wars and rumors of wars and violence throughout the world.

However, we are also seeing a growing movement for global peace and unity. Many are wrongly convinced that we are not headed for Armageddon, but we are about to usher in an age of peace and prosperity. Scripture indicates this false peace and unity will be short-lived.

Sexual Immorality

In spite of sexually transmitted diseases, unwanted pregnancies, and a host of other adverse consequences, sexual immorality is rampant in the world today. In fact, Scripture reveals it will only get worse. Revelation 9:21 makes known that during the Tribulation period people will not repent or give up their immorality.

Before God destroyed the world through the flood, we read in Genesis 6:5 —

The Lord saw how great man's wickedness on the earth had become, and that every inclination of the thoughts of his heart was only evil all the time.

What do we see today? A world given over to lust and every sexual perversion imaginable. We are living in a day and age when those who have restraint, discipline, and control, and who are not indulging in the lusts of the flesh, are considered to be in bondage. Those who lack self-control and have no inhibitions and are indulging in every lustful desire conceivable are believed to be liberated and free. We are seeing a reversal of values today like Isaiah 5:20 describes —

> Woe to those who call evil good and good evil, who put darkness for light and light for darkness ....

One of the main strategies of the enemy is to get people caught up in seeking pleasure and self-gratification. Then they have no time for God. They are too busy to study His Word and to see the signs of the times being fulfilled all around them. They are too occupied and insensitive to hear His voice convicting them of sin and bringing them to repentance.

Though the sexual immorality and perversion in the world today is alarming, what is even more alarming is how it has infiltrated many churches. God's enemy is intent on getting Christians involved in immorality. His goal is to neutralize (to render powerless and ineffective) believers in Christ and, ultimately, to destroy them and their testimonies.

People Won't Repent of Four Abominations

Revelation reveals that people in the last days — during the Tribulation — will refuse to repent of four main abominations:

1) Sorcery, Worshiping Demons, Idolatry —

   which means occultism and demonic phenomena will be very prominent.

2) Sexual Immorality —

   which means the world will be given over to lust and every sexual perversion imaginable.

3) Murders —

   which means it will be a very violent world.

4) Thefts/Lies —

which means deception, fraud, and corruption will be widespread.

Revelation 9:20,21 —

The rest of mankind that were not killed by these plagues still did not repent of the work of their hands; they did not stop worshiping demons, and idols of gold, silver, bronze, stone and wood — idols that cannot see or hear or walk. Nor did they repent of their murders, their magic arts [sorceries – KJV, NAS], their sexual immorality or their thefts.

Revelation 21:7, 8 —

He who overcomes will inherit all this, and I will be his God and he will be My son. But the cowardly, the unbelieving, the vile, the murderers, the sexually immoral, those who practice magic arts, the idolaters and all liars — their place will be in the fiery lake of burning sulfur. This is the second death.

Revelation 22:14,15 —

Blessed are those who wash their robes, that they may have the right to the tree of life and may go through the gates into the city. Outside are the dogs, those who practice magic arts, the sexually immoral, the murderers, the idolaters and everyone who loves and practices falsehood.

Israel

Another strong prophetic indicator is the nation of Israel. Throughout history numerous tyrannical rulers and hostile nations have persecuted and tried to annihilate the Jews, but God has miraculously preserved them.

For 2,500 years (since the Babylonian captivity), there had been no independent nation of Israel. The ten tribes of Israel, the northern kingdom, had been exiled to Assyria, 722 B.C.; they never returned as a nation. The remaining two tribes, the southern kingdom of Judah, went into Babylonian captivity in 586 B.C. when Nebuchadnezzar destroyed Jerusalem and the Temple. A small percentage of the captives returned to the land following a decree by Cyrus (536 B.C.) in fulfillment of Jeremiah's prophecy and rebuilt the Temple, but they were under Persian rule, and were later under the control of various other foreign nations.

A major scattering of Jews took place with the fall of Jerusalem in 70 A.D. and the defeat at Masada in 73 A.D. Many Jews fled Jerusalem at that time and also later in 135 A.D., when another Jewish revolt was crushed by the Romans. This is all part of the fulfillment of Jesus' prophecy in Matthew 23;37,38 —

> O Jerusalem, Jerusalem, you who kill the prophets and stone those sent to you, how often I have longed to gather your children together, as a hen gathers her chicks under her wings, but you were not willing. Look, your house is left to you desolate.

A small percentage of the Jewish people remained in the land under various foreign rulers, but most of the Jews had been scattered throughout the world. Yet the prophetic Scriptures promised a regathering and restoration of the Jewish people, and the prophets foretold that many events in the last days would focus in and around the tiny nation of Israel.

After nearly 1,900 years of worldwide dispersion, Israel became a nation on May 14, 1948. Modern day Israel is a miracle.

Amazing Survival

During a 1995 trip to Israel, I spent time on the Temple Mount in Jerusalem. One of the Moslem leaders told me that the Moslem world is going to unite and eradicate Israel, and push her into the sea. I asked, "When will that happen?" He said, "Very soon. When the time is right, we will unite. Israel will be forced to give us back Jerusalem, and we will get all of the West Bank and the Golan Heights." I have been on the Golan Heights. It overlooks the Galilee area. With Syria in control of the Golan Heights, Israel can be easily victimized, and without the West Bank, Israel would be hemmed in.

The nation's survival since May 14, 1948, has been truly amazing. On May 15, 1948, armies from neighboring Arab nations fought against Israeli defense forces. Israel, only one day old at the time, repelled the attack, and captured Arab territory. Jordan, however, still controlled East Jerusalem.

During the Six-Day War of June 5-10, 1967, the

greatly outnumbered Jews gained possession of the city of Jerusalem. The Jews were threatened with extermination by a combination of the surrounding Arab nations. In the ensuing conflict, Israel acquired both Sinai and East Jerusalem, as well as West Jordan.

I have been to Israel several times and have had opportunities to talk to various leaders and other people. They told of some of the miraculous occur-rences which had enabled them to survive when the odds were heavily against them. Some said, "We don't believe in Jesus as the Messiah. We don't even know if we believe in God, but what's happening over here — the way we have won battles and been protected — is almost like Bible days with David against Goliath." And they're right. God has an end-times purpose for events taking place there.

Rebuilding of the Temple

Before 1948 there was no nation of Israel. Today there is. Although the Temple has not yet been rebuilt in Jerusalem, I am convinced it will be — and sooner than many think.

Even as far back as 1984 when I was first in Israel, I discovered there were definite plans — kept relatively secret because they didn't want to cause a conflict with the Arab nations — to rebuild the Temple. Having been there several times since, I have seen these plans come to the forefront.

In 1995 I spent time in the Jewish quarter of Jerusalem. While there I attended a lecture and saw a presentation concerning plans to rebuild the Temple. I saw displays of artifacts and utensils — supposedly exact replicas of the originals — which are ready to be used in the future Temple. Once the Temple is rebuilt, the Jews can once again resume animal sacrifices and priestly offerings.

An orthodox Jewish rabbi told me that he was not

sure when the Temple would be rebuilt, but felt it would be in the not-too-distant future. I asked him, "What will you do with the Dome of the Rock?" His position was this: "When the time is right, the Moslems will let us dismantle the Dome of the Rock."

Another view that is held regarding the rebuilding of the Temple is that the Dome of the Rock is not located on the site of the former Temple. Many believe the Jewish Temple and the Dome of the Rock could coexist on the Temple Mount, with Jerusalem being the religious capital of the world.

However it occurs, I definitely believe that the Temple will be rebuilt and that the Antichrist is going to desecrate it.

Archaeological excavations have been carried on by the Department of Antiquities of Hebrew University for some years. Archaeological explorations have been done beneath the Temple Mount. Measurements have also been made on the Temple Mount, with the view to rebuilding the Temple.

I have been back to Jerusalem several times since 1995 — spending many days in the Jewish quarter attending lectures, researching, and interacting with rabbis and other leaders. I have noticed an increasing desire and progression toward the eventual rebuilding of the Temple as prophesied in Scripture.

There is a growing desire for rebuilding the Temple on the Temple Mount in Jerusalem and restoring the ritual sacrifices. More and more Jews are longing for the Messiah to rebuild the Temple and restore the Davidic kingdom to its former power and glory. They await the Messiah to come and usher in the Messianic kingdom wherein: the dead will be resurrected, death and disease will be eradicated, the millennial Temple will be rebuilt, Judah and Israel will be reunited, there will be universal peace and prosperity (even the animals will live in peace and harmony), the whole earth will be filled with the knowledge of the Lord and the Torah, and the commandments will be obeyed.

Desecration of the Temple

Scripture indicates that in the middle of the seven-year Tribulation period the Antichrist will desecrate the Temple, proclaiming himself to be God. He will place an image of himself in the Temple and command individuals to worship it. This is the "abomination that causes desolation" spoken of in Daniel 9:27, and which Jesus referred to in Matthew 24:15. Paul also mentions in II Thessalonians 2:4 that the Antichrist "sets himself up in God's temple, proclaiming himself to be God." John, in Revelation 13:14,15, reveals that an image set up in honor of the Antichrist will be given breath so that it can speak and that all who refuse to worship the image will be killed.

Many Jews will be deceived into believing that the Antichrist is their Messiah. However, when he desecrates the Temple and demands worship, they will then know he is an imposter. Then the Antichrist will initiate the worst persecution of the Jews in the history of the world. Matthew 24:15-22 warns —

> So when you see standing in the holy place "the abomination that causes desolation," spoken of through the prophet Daniel — let the reader understand — then let those who are in Judea flee to the mountains. Let no one on the roof of his house go down to take anything out of the house. Let no one in the field go back to get his cloak. How dreadful it will be in those days for pregnant woman and nursing mothers! Pray that your flight will not take place in winter or on the Sabbath. For then there will be great distress, unequaled from the beginning of the world until now — and never to be equaled again. If those days had not been cut short, no one

would survive, but for the sake of the elect those days will be shortened.

Jews Rejected the True Messiah

The Jews rejected their true Messiah, but the Bible says they will temporarily accept a counterfeit. Jesus states in John 5:43 —

I have come in My Father's name, and you do not accept Me; but if someone else comes in his own name, you will accept him.

The Jews will initially believe the Antichrist is the Messiah, and what they think to be the Millennium will turn out to be their Great Tribulation.

Daniel 12:1-3 states —

At that time Michael, the great prince who protects your people, will arise. There will be a time of distress such as has not happened from the beginning of nations until then. But at that time your people — everyone whose name is found written in the book — will be delivered. Multitudes who sleep in the dust of the earth will awake: some to everlasting life, others to shame and everlasting contempt. Those who are wise will shine like the brightness of the heavens, and those who lead many to righteousness, like the stars for ever and ever.

We get a glimpse of how great this deception will be when we look at Malachi 4:5,6, which states —

See, I will send you the prophet Elijah before that great and dreadful day of the Lord comes. He will turn the hearts of the fathers to their children, and the hearts of the children to their fathers; or else I will come and strike the land with a curse.

When we look back at I Kings 18:38, we see that the fire of the Lord fell and consumed Elijah's sacrifice. We also discover in the first chapter of II Kings that on two occasions Elijah called down fire from heaven to consume a captain and his company of 50 men. Fire also came out from the presence of the Lord to consume the burnt offering as Moses and Aaron stood before the Tent of Meeting (Leviticus 9:23,24). How easy it will be for the Jews to be deceived into thinking the False Prophet, who will cause "fire to come down from heaven to earth in full view of men" (Revelation 13:13), is Elijah who is expected to come before the great and dreadful day of the Lord.

This potential for deception gets even greater. There are many Jewish views of the nature and mission of the Messiah. One of these views, I feel, adds significance to our study.

Some rabbinical scholars believe that two Messiahs will appear — one after the other. One will be named Messiah ben (son of) Joseph and the other Messiah ben (son of) David. Messiah ben Joseph dies leading wars against Gog and Magog and his body is left on the streets of Jerusalem for forty days. Jewish legend then relates that Messiah ben David appears and resuscitates Messiah ben Joseph. This Messiah ben David will go on to have victory over the armies of Gog and Magog.*

Let's consider this particular Jewish perspective on the Messiah in light of Biblical prophecy. Think about what is going to happen when the Antichrist appears. Revelation 13:3 talks about a deadly wound and the world's astonishment at the miraculous recovery of the Antichrist from this fatal wound. Revelation 13:11 brings the False Prophet onto the scene performing great and miraculous signs and pointing the worship of all people to the Antichrist. The Bible indicates that the Temple in Jerusalem is to be rebuilt and the Antichrist is sure to win the

---

* *The Messiah Texts*, Raphael Patai, (Wayne State University Press, Detroit) 1979, pp. xxxiii, xxxiv.

acceptance of the Jews by having a part in this. He will usher in a seven-year peace treaty allowing Jerusalem to become his world capital of religion. This is the scenario developing on the world scene. Many Jewish people will be deceived and accept this Antichrist as their Messiah partly because what is happening fits in with Messianic views already in place in Jewish writings.

Through counterfeit miracles and strong delusion, the Antichrist will be temporarily honored as the promised Messiah, the Savior of the world. Revelation 11:8 refers to Jerusalem as "Sodom and Egypt" since it will be filled with immorality and sorcery due to the Antichrist's regime.

Although Israel as a nation has rejected Jesus as the Messiah, a remnant has always known Him. Revelation 7 indicates that during the Tribulation 144,000 from all the tribes of Israel will be redeemed. It appears from the context that these Jewish believers will preach the Gospel of Jesus Christ throughout the world during the Tribulation and bear much fruit for His glory.

Multi-National Force

When I spoke to the U.S. military officers and enlisted men on a military base in Germany in 1990, I asked, "When in the history of the world has a multi-national force ever surrounded a country which was not being aggressive toward them?" They responded, "Never." I said, "What we are witnessing with Iraq is a steppingstone to the fulfillment of prophecies by Zechariah."

Just as many nations of the world gathered their military forces around Iraq to enforce an economic embargo, it was prophesied in Scripture thousands of years ago that all the nations of the world would be gathered against Jerusalem (Zechariah 12:3).

One day a multi-national force representing a

global society is going to fight against Jerusalem. Zechariah 14:2 states —

I will gather all the nations to Jerusalem to fight against it; the city will be captured, the houses ransacked, and the women raped. Half of the city will go into exile, but the rest of the people will not be taken from the city.

The Deliverer Will Come

Just when it appears that all is lost, the Deliverer, the Messiah of Israel, will return from heaven with the saints of God and overthrow the enemies of Israel. He will establish His Kingdom and rule the world in righteousness.

Zechariah 14:3-9 states —

Then the Lord will go out and fight against those nations, as He fights in the day of battle. On that day His feet will stand on the Mount of Olives, east of Jerusalem, and the Mount of Olives will be split in two from east to west, forming a great valley, with half of the mountain moving north and half moving south. You will flee by my mountain valley, for it will extend to Azel. You will flee as you fled from the earthquake in the days of Uzziah king of Judah. Then the Lord my God will come, and all the holy ones with Him.

On that day there will be no light, no cold or frost. It will be a unique day, without daytime or nighttime — a day known to the Lord. When evening comes, there will be light. On that day living water will flow out from Jerusalem, half to the eastern sea and half to the western sea, in summer and in winter. The Lord will be king over the whole earth. On that day there will be one Lord, and His name the only name.

When Yeshua (Jesus) returns, the Jews will mourn because they will realize that they had rejected their true Messiah. Consider the following Scriptures:

Zechariah 12:10 —

And I will pour out on the house of David and the inhabitants of Jerusalem a spirit of grace and supplication. They will look on Me, the One they have pierced, and they will mourn for Him as one mourns for an only child, and grieve bitterly for Him as one grieves for a firstborn son.

Matthew 24:30 —

At that time the sign of the Son of Man will appear in the sky, and all the nations of the earth will mourn. They will see the Son of Man coming on the clouds of the sky, with power and great glory.

Revelation 1:7 —

Look, He is coming with the clouds, and every eye will see Him, even those who pierced Him; and all the peoples of the earth will mourn because of Him. So shall it be! Amen.

The final question Jesus answers before His ascension as recorded in Acts 1:6-8 implies that at some future date He will restore the kingdom to Israel —

So when they met together, they asked Him, "Lord, are You at this time going to restore the kingdom to Israel?" He said to them: "It is not for you to know the times or dates the Father has set by his own authority. But you will receive power when the Holy Spirit comes on you; and you will be My witnesses in Jerusalem, and in all Judea and Samaria, and to the ends of the earth."

Peter speaks to the Jews in Acts 3:17-21 —

Now, brothers, I know that you acted in ignorance, as did your leaders. But this is how God fulfilled what He had foretold through all the prophets, saying that His Christ would suffer. Repent, then, and turn to God, so that your sins may be wiped out, that times of refreshing may come from the Lord, and that He may send the Christ, who has been appointed for you — even Jesus. He must remain in heaven until the time comes for God to restore everything, as He promised long ago through His holy prophets.

In Romans 11:25-27, Paul states —

I do not want you to be ignorant of this mystery, brothers, so that you may not be conceited: Israel has experienced a hardening in part until the full number of the Gentiles has come in. And so all Israel will be saved, as it is written: "The deliverer will come from Zion; He will turn godlessness away from Jacob. And this is My covenant with them when I take away their sins."

There will be a scattering of the Jewish people in the middle of the Tribulation period when the Antichrist desecrates the Temple. The final gathering will be when Messiah Yeshua returns to establish His Kingdom. Mark 13:26,27 tells us —

At that time men will see the Son of Man coming in clouds with great power and glory. And He will send His angels and gather His elect from the four winds, from the ends of the earth to the ends of the heavens.

Jesus' prophecy in Matthew 23:39 will be fulfilled —

For I tell you, you will not see Me again until you say, "Blessed is He who comes in the name of the Lord."

Millennial Promises Fulfilled

During the Millennium, the prophecies and promises concerning possession of the land will be fulfilled, the Temple of Ezekiel's prophetic vision will be built. The presence of the Lord, which in Ezekiel's vision progressively departed from the Temple in Jerusalem because of Israel's sins (Ezekiel chapters 8-11), fills the millennial Temple and the earth (Ezekiel 43:1-5). The nations will have a knowledge of the Lord as He rules and reigns from Jerusalem.

Ezekiel 37:11-28 —

Then He said to me: "Son of man, these bones are the whole house of Israel. They say, 'Our bones are dried up and our hope is gone; we are cut off.' Therefore prophesy and say to them: ' This is what the Sovereign Lord says: O my people, I am going to open your graves and bring you up from them; I will bring you back to the land of Israel. Then you, My people, will know that I am the Lord, when I open your graves and bring you up from them. I will put My Spirit in you and you will live, and I will settle you in your own land. Then you will know that I the Lord have spoken, and I have done it, declares the Lord. ...

I will take the Israelites out of the nations where they have gone. I will gather them from all around and bring them back into their own land. I will make them one nation in the land, on the mountains of Israel. There will be one king over all of them and they will never again be two nations or be divided into two kingdoms. They will no longer defile themselves with their idols and vile images or with any of their offenses, for I will save them from all their sinful backsliding, and I will cleanse them. They will be My people, and I will be their God.

'My servant David will be king over them, and they will all have one shepherd. They will follow My laws and be careful to keep My decrees. They will live in the land I gave to My servant Jacob, the land where your fathers lived. They and their children and their children's children will live there forever, and David My servant will be their prince forever. I will make a covenant of peace with them; it will be an everlasting covenant. I will establish them and increase their numbers, and I will put My sanctuary among them forever. My dwelling place will be with them; I will be their God, and they will be My people. Then the nations will know that I the Lord make Israel holy, when My sanctuary is among them forever.' "

Zechariah 14:11,16 —

It [Jerusalem] will be inhabited; never again will it be destroyed. Jerusalem will be secure. Then the survivors from all the nations that have attacked Jerusalem will go up year after year to worship the King, the Lord Almighty, and to celebrate the Feast of Tabernacles.

Isaiah 2:2-5 —

In the last days the mountain of the Lord's Temple will be established as chief among the mountains; it will be raised above the hills, and all nations will stream to it. Many peoples will come and say, "Come, let us go up to the mountain of the Lord, to the house of the God of Jacob. He will teach us His ways, so that we may walk in His paths." The law will go out from Zion, the word of the Lord from Jerusalem.

He will judge between the nations and will settle disputes for many peoples. They will beat their swords into plowshares and their spears into pruning hooks. Nation will not take up sword against nation, nor will they train for war anymore. Come, O house of Jacob, let us walk in the light of the Lord.

Isaiah 11:6-9 —

The wolf will live with the lamb, the leopard will lie down with the goat, the calf and the lion and the yearling together; and a little child will lead them. The cow will feed with the bear, their young will lie down together, and the lion will eat straw like the ox. The infant will play near the hole of the cobra, and the young child put his hand into the viper's nest. They will neither harm nor destroy on all My holy mountain, for the earth will be full of the knowledge of the Lord as the waters cover the sea.

Isaiah 60:1-20 —

Arise, shine, for your light has come, and the glory of the Lord rises upon you ....

Nations will come to your light, and kings to the brightness of your dawn .... Then you will look and be radiant, your heart will throb and swell with joy; the wealth on the seas will be brought to you, to you the riches of the nations will come ....

Your gates will always stand open, they will never be shut, day or night, so that men may bring you the wealth of the nations — their kings led in triumphal procession ....

No longer will violence be heard in your land, nor ruin or destruction within your borders, but you will call your walls Salvation and your gates Praise. The sun will no more be your light by day, nor will the brightness of the moon shine on you, for the Lord will be your everlasting light, and your God will be your glory. Your sun will never set again, and your moon will wane no more; the Lord will be your everlasting light, and your days of sorrow will end.

Isaiah 65:19-25 —

I will rejoice over Jerusalem and take delight in My people; the sound of weeping and of crying will be heard in it no more. Never again will there be in it an infant who lives but a few days, or an old man who does not live out his years; he who dies at a hundred will be thought a mere youth; he who fails to reach a hundred will be considered accursed.

They will build houses and dwell in them; they will plant vineyards and eat their fruit. No longer will they build houses and others live in them, or plant and others eat. For as the days of a tree, so will be the days of My people; My chosen ones will long enjoy the works of their hands.

They will not toil in vain or bear children doomed to misfortune; for they will be a people blessed by the Lord, they and their descendants with them. Before they call I will answer; while they are still speaking I will hear.

The wolf and the lamb will feed together, and the lion will eat straw like the ox ....

Jeremiah 31:31-34 —

"The time is coming," declares the Lord, "when I will make a new covenant with the house of Israel and with the house of Judah. It will not be like the covenant I made with their forefathers when I took them by the hand to lead them out of Egypt, because they broke My covenant, though I was a husband to them," declares the Lord.

"This is the covenant I will make with the house of Israel after that time," declares the Lord. "I will put My law in their minds and write it on their hearts. I will be their God, and they will be My people. No longer will a man teach his neighbor, or a man his brother, saying, 'Know the Lord,' because they will all know Me, from the least of them to the greatest," declares the Lord. "For I will forgive their wickedness and will remember their sins no more."

Micah 4:5-8 —

... we will walk in the name of the Lord our God for ever and ever. "In that day," declares the Lord, "I will gather the lame; I will assemble the exiles and those I have brought to grief. I will make the lame a remnant, those driven away a strong nation. The Lord will rule over them in Mount Zion from that day and for ever. As for you, O watchtower of the flock, O stronghold of the Daughter of Zion, the former dominion will be restored to you; kingship will come to the Daughter of Jerusalem."

Zechariah 8:23 —

This is what the Lord Almighty says: "In those days ten men from all languages and nations will take firm hold of one Jew by the hem of his robe and say, 'Let us go with you, because we have heard that God is with you.'"

More Amazing Prophecies

There are many amazing prophecies in Scripture that confirm divine inspiration. The following are just a few more to consider.

The Earth Will Be Burned Up

II Peter 3:8-13 states —

But do not let this one fact escape your notice, beloved, that with the Lord one day is as a thousand years, and a thousand years as one day. The Lord is not slow about His promise, as some count slowness, but is patient toward you, not wishing for any to perish but for all to come to repentance.

But the day of the Lord will come like a thief, in which the heavens will pass away with a roar and the elements will be destroyed with intense heat, and the earth and its works will be burned up.

Since all these things are to be destroyed in this way, what sort of people ought you to be in holy conduct and godliness, looking for and hastening the coming of the day of God, on account of which the heavens will be destroyed by burning, and the elements will melt with intense heat! But according to His promise we are looking for new heavens and a new earth, in which righteousness dwells (NAS).

These verses were once used by skeptics to disprove the Bible. How could there be a fire big enough to burn the whole world? Many scientists laughed at these verses before World War II, but after Hiroshima and the advent of nuclear weapons which can actually melt the basic building blocks of matter itself, many began to see the potential for the fulfillment of these prophecies — even separate from God's supernatural intervention. The nuclear weapons today are many times more powerful than the two bombs which destroyed Hiroshima and Nagasaki in 1945.

Flesh Will Rot

Zechariah 14:12 warns —

This is the plague with which the Lord will strike all the nations that fought against Jerusalem: Their flesh will rot while they are still standing on their feet, their eyes will rot in their sockets, and their tongues will rot in their mouths.

Although this could in fact refer to a supernatural judgment by the Lord, it is interesting to realize that we now have nuclear weapons that could cause the very fulfillment of this verse. While prophecies such as this in Zechariah 14:12 were hard to comprehend not too many years ago, they no longer sound like science fiction.

The Two Witnesses

What about the two witnesses who will prophesy for 1,260 days?

Revelation 11:3-12 —

And I will give power to My two witnesses, and they will prophesy for 1,260 days, clothed in sackcloth. These are the two olive trees and the two lamp stands that stand before the Lord of the earth. If anyone tries to harm them, fire comes from their mouths and devours their enemies. This is how anyone who wants to harm them must die. These men have power to shut up the sky so that it will not rain during the time they are prophesying; and they have power to turn the waters into blood and to strike the earth with every kind of plague as often as they want.

Now when they have finished their testimony, the beast that comes up from the Abyss will attack them, and overpower and kill them. Their bodies will lie in the street of the great city, which is figuratively called Sodom and Egypt, where also their Lord was crucified. For three and a half days men from every people, tribe, language and nation will gaze on their bodies and refuse them burial. The inhabitants of the earth will gloat over them and will celebrate by sending each other gifts, because these two prophets had tormented those who live on the earth.

But after the three and a half days a breath of life from God entered them, and they stood on their feet, and terror struck those who saw them. Then they heard a loud voice from heaven saying to them, "Come up here." And they went up to heaven in a cloud, while their enemies looked on.

For centuries people were baffled by these verses which describe God's two witnesses lying in the streets of Jerusalem (after being killed by the Antichrist) as people from all nations of the world look upon their dead bodies. How could someone back in the first century A.D. accurately predict this universal viewing by his own inspiration? With the use of satellite and internet technology this prophecy can now be fulfilled.

I have been in many villages around the world. Some of the places were so remote that the people I encountered stared at my skin and blue eyes, because they had never seen a white person in real life. Yet even in secluded areas there has often been someone who had a television. I have seen many people gathered around the television — whether it was in a hotel, business, or someone's house — to watch events on the news as they occurred around the world. There is a widespread awareness that some amazing things are happening on the world scene. Those who are believers in Christ know that prophecy is being fulfilled and the Lord's return is close at hand.

It is also interesting to note that, although the two witnesses are from God and empowered by Him, the world will be so undiscerning and unrepentant that they will despise and reject them. When the Antichrist is finally able to kill the two witnesses (only when their testimony for God is finished), the people — so deep in rebellion against the God of the Bible — will rejoice over their deaths and celebrate by exchanging gifts.

Mark of the Beast

The book of Revelation reveals that there is a day coming when people won't be able to buy or sell without a mark on the right hand or forehead. Revelation 13:16-18 —

He also forced everyone, small and great, rich and poor, free and slave, to receive a mark on his right hand or on his forehead, so that no one could buy or sell unless he had the mark, which is the name of the beast or the number of his name. This calls for wisdom. If anyone has insight, let him calculate the number of the beast, for it is man's number. His number is 666.

For almost 2,000 years this Scripture did not make sense, and until several years ago, it still did not seem feasible.

For instance, in 1971, when I first became a Christian, I shared with a friend about last days Biblical prophecies. He laughed and said it could never happen. I said, "Well then, at least remember this. Don't ever take a mark on your right hand or forehead." He responded, "If that ever happens, I will not take the mark of the beast. I will then know the

Bible is God's Word and Revelation is true."

My friend is now very close to realizing that God's Word and Revelation are true. Technology has advanced far enough to completely fulfill Revelation 13:16-18.

Keep in mind that John's Revelation was recorded nearly 2,000 years ago when the basic weapons were swords and spears, and the communication system was written words and face-to-face conversation. Yet the apostle John, under the anointing of the Holy Spirit, prophesied with precise detail the world system that you and I are seeing develop before our very eyes.

We have the technology, not just to imprint a number on human flesh, but to implant an ultra-thin microchip with considerable data to be read by an electronic scanning device. The Antichrist, not having infinite knowledge like God, will have at his disposal the technology to monitor every human being on this planet, thus giving him apparent omniscience.

The Beast's Image

Revelation 13:14,15, reveals that an image set up in honor of the Antichrist will be given breath so that it can speak and that all who refuse to worship the image will be killed. It states —

> Because of the signs he [False Prophet] was given power to do on behalf of the first beast [Antichrist], he deceived the inhabitants of the earth. He ordered them to set up an image in honor of the beast who was wounded by the sword and yet lived. He was given power to give breath to the image of the first beast, so that it could speak and cause all who refused to worship the image to be killed.

As I watched the image of a man being projected on a large screen before a vast auditorium of people to whom he was speaking, it occurred to me that this is one possible method for the fulfillment of Revelation 13:15 concerning giving breath to the image of the Antichrist. Without discounting the possibility of counterfeit miracles, advanced computer technology combined with biomechanical or virtual reality technology make possible many other potential fulfillments of this once perplexing prophecy. Robots are being created in the field of artificial intelligence. Mechanical and electrical components are used to simulate living creatures in animatronics. Also, voice recognition systems, 3-D replicas, holograms, and interactive visual environments are all intriguing possibilities. In such an interactive electronic world, we can now understand how it is possible for an image to appear to be alive, be able to speak, and even determine whether we are worshipping it or not.

The Beast's Mark

Cash can be counterfeited, checks can be forged, and credit cards can be stolen, so the ultimate solution is what Revelation foretells: a mark on the right hand or forehead for the exchange of goods and services.

Do you know how hard it is to rent or buy certain items today without a credit card? It is virtually impossible to rent cars, book airline tickets, reserve hotel rooms, or order items without a credit card.

There is nothing wrong with credit cards in themselves (unless you overcharge or pay interest). However, credit cards, debit cards, smart cards, and other devices will become outdated, leading to a predominantly cashless system. No one will be able to buy or sell without a mark on the right hand or forehead. Those who refuse this mark will face possible starvation, unemployment, persecution, and eventual martyrdom.

You might ask, "Who would take the mark of the beast?" I remember back in the '70s when I was going to Bible college in Ohio. There was supposedly a gas shortage, so people would line up for blocks to get their rationed amount. If someone cut in line, people would become violent — doing almost anything to get their gas. To what extreme will people go to save their jobs, their lives, and their families from starvation?

By distorting the context of verses such as Ezekiel 9:3-6 and Revelation 7:3 and 14:1, some of those taking the mark of the beast (Revelation 13) may be led to believe that they are actually taking a mark from and for the Lord.

How will one be able to differentiate between the seal of God and the mark of the beast? Only by knowing the Word of God and the Jesus of the Bible. Therefore, Scriptural insight and spiritual discernment are invaluable.

I recently talked to a Christian concerning the mark of the beast and its dangers according to Revelation. To my amazement, this Christian thought that the mark was a good idea because a cashless society and one-world government will benefit humanity. He reasoned that God would never be opposed to something apparently good. When I told him to examine what Revelation had to say on the subject, he said he didn't have time to read the Bible.

God's Irrevocable Judgment

I used to wonder why God's judgment would be so severe and irrevocable for someone merely taking a mark on their hand or forehead. Revelation 14:9-11 warns —

> A third angel followed them and said in a loud voice: "If anyone worships the beast and his image and receives his mark on the forehead or on the hand, he, too, will drink of the wine of God's fury, which has been poured full strength into the cup of His wrath. He will be tormented with burning sulfur in the presence of the holy angels and of the Lamb. And the smoke of their

torment rises for ever and ever. There is no rest day or night for those who worship the beast and his image, or for anyone who receives the mark of his name."

Obviously, there must be more to the mark than just an identification symbol for a world society. I think that on the surface, their philosophy will be that if you are a good citizen of the world and want global peace and prosperity, then you will identify with it by taking this mark. In order to avert a potential economic catastrophe, a universal identification system will be imposed. Many will take it for the sole purpose of financial security, thereby rejecting the Lord as the rich young ruler did in Luke 18:18-24.

I am convinced, however, that the brief glimpse Scripture gives concerning this mark reveals there is much more to it. I believe that to take this mark will in reality be a renunciation of faith in the Jesus Christ of the Bible, an acceptance of the counterfeit Messiah, and an initiation into the very religion and worldwide rule of the Antichrist.

Revelation indicates that those who take this mark may have convenience initially. However, they will pay a far greater price later when God's wrath and judgment is meted out on a rebellious world and apostate church. It will far exceed the price paid by those who are persecuted and martyred by the Antichrist for refusing to take his mark.

Global Society

Revelation 13:7 and Daniel 7:23 prophesy about the establishment of a world government. For over twenty years (when it seemed impossible to be fulfilled) I have been saying that we are heading toward a unified global society with a one-world government, a one-world monetary system, and a one-world religion. Most people said, "You're crazy! It will never happen!" But guess what? Those people aren't saying that anymore. Now they're saying, "Oh, we knew it was inevitable."

Years ago everyone thought the world was too divided and that there was no way to break down national, social, racial, cultural, political, economic, religious, and territorial barriers. But Scripture has revealed, and research has confirmed, that we are heading toward a unified global society.

Potential Worldwide Crises

People throughout the world have been hearing through the media for years about crises, whether actual, potential, or fabricated. A partial and growing list includes:

- the threat of nuclear holocaust
- violence and ethnic hostility
- overpopulation
- economic catastrophe
- worldwide famine and mass starvation
- strange and out-of-control weather conditions
- water, land, and air pollution
- global warming
- destruction of the tropical rain forests
- epidemic infectious diseases

These and many other things have caused the world's political and religious leaders to say, "We are not merely dealing with national crises; we are facing global catastrophes. Therefore, we must unite for the common good of the world. We must lay down our personal interests for the good of the group; we must lay down our group's interest for the good of the nation; and we must lay down our national interests for the good of all humanity and our global society."

This is all setting the stage for the ultimate fulfillment of what God foretold in Revelation and in numerous other Biblical prophecies.

West/East Germany Border Events

We have seen some incredible things happen at an accelerated speed:

• The Berlin Wall Came Down:

I asked an officer in U.S. Army Intelligence, who had participated in military maneuvers near the former West Germany/East Germany border, when he had found out the Berlin Wall was coming down. He replied, "The very day it happened!" They had no idea it would come down. That's how fast things progressed.

While I was ministering in Germany in 1990 (then it was West Germany), we went on a border tour. We visited a place nicknamed "Little Berlin," which is about 10 km north of the city of Hof. I stood on the East German border where a few months earlier I would have been shot by East German border guards. I saw two farms which were previously on opposite sides of the wall, separated for nearly 40 years. The owners, who were brothers, for decades could only see each other and wave from a distance.

• The Fall of Communism in the Soviet Union:

After this I was taken into Czechoslovakia, a former communist country. While waiting to cross the border I saw a sign that said, "Czechoslovakia — Socialist Republic," but "Socialist" was scratched out.

• East and West Germany Reunited:

Even with the Berlin Wall and the Iron Curtain removed, world leaders could not believe Germany would unite for many years, if ever. But it happened. The politicians were speechless, and the news media could barely keep up with the unexpected developments as East and West Germany became one nation.

The Soviet empire has been dismantled. The kings of the East are preparing. Alliances are being made which could fulfill Ezekiel chapters 38 and 39. A new world order is imminent. Signs of the revived Roman Empire through a unified European Community are evident. Even as you read this book, we are moving closer to the uniting of the world on a global scale and to the reign of the Antichrist and False Prophet.

Unity of Religion

The Bible speaks of a new age of love, unity, peace, and prosperity after Christ returns to this earth to rule and reign. It repeatedly warns, however, that before the true Millennium on earth and the new heavens and new earth, there will be a temporary false peace and unity on a worldwide level, culminating in unified worship, political power, and economic control. This occult-empowered system of delusion and oppression is referred to as Babylon the Great.

Main Descriptive Word — Deception

The main descriptive word of the last days is deception. Scripture warns repeatedly of an unprecedented time of deception and delusion. The world will be offered false prophets, false miracles, false teachings, a false revival, a false Messiah, a false peace, and a false unity.

Jesus warned about false prophets and false Christs in Matthew 24:4,5,11,24 —

Watch out that no one deceives you. For many will come in My name, claiming, "I am the Christ," and will deceive many. And many false prophets will appear and deceive many people. For false Christs and false prophets will appear and perform great signs and miracles to deceive even the elect — if that were possible.

Paul cautioned about the apostasy and counterfeit miracles, signs, and wonders in II Thessalonians 2:3, 9-12 —

> Don't let anyone deceive you in any way, for that day will not come until the rebellion [apostasy, falling away] occurs and the man of lawlessness is revealed, the man doomed to destruction. The coming of the lawless one will be in accordance with the work of Satan displayed in all kinds of counterfeit miracles, signs and wonders, and in every sort of evil that deceives those who are perishing. They perish because they refused to love the truth and so be saved. For this reason God sends them a powerful delusion so that they will believe the lie and so that all will be condemned who have not believed the truth but have delighted in wickedness.

Paul also warned about deceitful spirits and doctrines of demons in I Timothy 4:1 —

> The Spirit clearly says that in later times some will abandon the faith and follow deceiving spirits and things taught by demons.

Paul reveals there will be those who will not endure sound doctrine, but will want to have their ears tickled. II Timothy 4:3,4 states —

> For the time will come when men will not put up with sound doctrine. Instead, to suit their own desires, they will gather around them a great number of teachers to say what their itching ears want to hear. They will turn their ears away from the truth and turn aside to myths.

In Revelation 13:13,14; 19:20, John warns about the whole earth being deceived because of the signs the False Prophet performs in the presence of the Antichrist —

And he performed great and miraculous signs, even causing fire to come down from heaven to earth in full view of men. Because of the signs he [False Prophet] was given power to do on behalf of the first beast [Antichrist], he deceived the inhabitants of the earth. He ordered them to set up an image in honor of the beast who was wounded by the sword and yet lived. But the beast was captured, and with him the false prophet who had performed the miraculous signs on his behalf. With these signs he had deluded those who had received the mark of the beast and worshiped his image.

The "two horns like a lamb" (Revelation 13:11) seems to indicate the False Prophet's imitation of the true Lamb, Jesus Christ. The False Prophet's deception is intensified because of its similarity to the truth. Jesus warned in Matthew 7:15 —

Watch out for false prophets. They come to you in sheep's clothing, but inwardly they are ferocious wolves.

Two Opposite Unities

For many years I have seen two unities on the horizon. Now they are rapidly coming into formation.

There is a unity of true believers in Christ — those committed to Biblical Christianity. This Scripturally based unity consists of those who have accepted Jesus Christ as Savior and Lord; believe He is the promised Messiah, God incarnate, and the only way of salvation; believe in salvation through faith because of His shed blood and resurrection; and are not involving themselves in unscriptural beliefs, practices, and phenomena which are sweeping the apostate church.

They are walking in obedience to God's Word and Spirit. These Biblical Christians have unity of the "faith that was once for all entrusted to the saints" (Jude 3).

There is also a growing unity of delusion and deception on a level the world has never seen before. I warned about its coming for many years, and now it is happening. The current false unity movement is rapidly merging apostate Christianity and New Ageism to achieve its ultimate goals. These goals include such humanly appealing concepts as global unity, a worldwide celebration of peace and joy, the achieving of individual godhood, cleansing the earth of all evil, and the establishing of "God's Kingdom." Revelation 13:8 gives the ultimate end of this counterfeit love and unity —

> All inhabitants of the earth will worship the beast [Antichrist] — all whose names have not been written in the book of life ....

Occultism, Eastern mysticism, the New Age movement, and the human potential movement are all coming together. They are basically the same, teaching that man is the measure of all things and that you and I are gods; all we have to do is achieve god consciousness. They teach that there is no sin — so there is no need for a crucified and resurrected Savior. All we need is love and unity. Join all that together with apostate Christianity, which is proclaiming a popular message to the masses of love and unity, and you have what I believe will be the religious system that the coming Antichrist and False Prophet will use to deceive the world.

The world's religions will have no problem uniting with a watered-down Christianity based on love and unity, and signs and wonders.

In the Old Testament, Babylon was the center of occultism (Isaiah 47). Babylon represented a pagan culture rebellious against God, wicked, immoral, proud, and haughty, trusting in their own wisdom, sorceries, and spells. John identifies the great prostitute, the religious system prophesied in Revelation chapter 17, as Babylon the Great. It is interesting that the New Ageism and apostate Christianity of today closely resemble the description of Babylon in the Old Testament and Revelation. We are seeing a revival of occultism and sorcery today which is infiltrating every aspect of society: education, science, environmentalism, medicine, health, psychology, politics, and religion — in virtually every nation of the world.

Similar Mystical Experiences

It is amazing to discover how people around the globe are having similar mystical experiences: someone in India through meditation; someone in the U.S. using hallucinogenic drugs such as peyote to have a vision; someone in British Columbia through trance channeling; someone in Europe through a seance; someone in Africa or Haiti through voodoo; and even a professing Christian experiencing bizarre phenomena and "new revelations" supposedly attributed to the Holy Spirit. They all are having encounters with spirit entities (claiming to be angels, Jesus, the Holy Spirit, aliens, and so on), which are teaching them that we are gods, that we must remove all barriers and unite on a global scale to save our planet, and that a great world leader is about to come on the scene who is going to usher in a new world order, an enlightened age of spiritual unity and peace — a virtual utopia.

Generation Raised on Occultism

We are seeing a generation of young people and adults being programmed, seduced, and deceived. They have been raised on a diet of occultism and supernatural phenomena and powers through cartoons, movies, music, videos, and games. Then tie in subliminal motivation, mind-altering and hallucinogenic drugs, and mind-expansion techniques for achieving altered states of consciousness. No wonder Paul prophesied that a "powerful delusion" will overtake the world (II Thessalonians 2:11).

Think about how easily these people will be deceived when the one whose coming "will be in accordance with the work of Satan displayed in all kinds of counterfeit miracles, signs and wonders" (II Thessalonians 2:9). He will perform "great and miraculous signs, even causing fire to come down from heaven to earth in full view of men" (Revelation 13:13). Revelation 13:8 states —

> All inhabitants of the earth will worship the beast — all whose names have not been written in the book of life belonging to the Lamb that was slain from the creation of the world.

Satanic Trinity

Throughout history Satan has attempted to mimic the true God of creation. Therefore it is not surprising that soon to be revealed is Satan's imitation of the divine Trinity. In order for a counterfeit to be accepted and propagated in the world it has to be very close to the original.

The satanic trinity consists of:

• The Dragon (Satan) counterfeiting God the Father.

• The beast (coming out of the sea – Revelation 13:1) or Antichrist, receiving authority from the Dragon (Revelation 13:4), counterfeiting Jesus Christ and pretending to be the Messiah. Just as Jesus died and rose again, so Satan will have his false Messiah appear to die and rise from the dead (Revelation 13:3,14; 17:8,11).

• And the False Prophet, sometimes referred to as the second beast (coming out of the earth – Revelation 13:11), counterfeiting the work of the Holy Spirit and leading the world to worship the Antichrist (Revelation 13:11-18).

Revelation 16:13 says —

Then I saw three evil spirits that looked like frogs; they came out of the mouth of the dragon, out of the mouth of the beast and out of the mouth of the false prophet.

God describes Satan as a dragon and the Antichrist and the False Prophet as beasts. God uses these words to indicate their true nature and intent, but the world will not initially see them that way. Deceived by surface appearance, the people of the world will believe the Antichrist and False Prophet to be godly, when in fact they are extremely evil.

Revelation 9:1-11 is a vivid description of unrestrained demonic activity on the earth in the last days. Those who are involved in sorcery, magic arts, idolatry, occultism, and New Ageism would do well to consider the account of the demonic beings released from the abyss. The true intent of Satan and his demonic cohorts is to inflict harm, torture, and destruction on human beings — even those in allegiance with him.

The satanic principalities and powers were defeated at the cross (John 12:31, 16:11; Colossians 2:15), but do continue their evil deception and influences in the present age (Ephesians 2:2, I Thessalonians 3:5; I Peter 5:8,9; Revelation 2:10) until they are stripped of all power at Christ's return.

Antichrist Appears to Be Messiah

I believe "the lie" Paul talks about in II Thessalonians 2:11 ultimately refers to the Antichrist "proclaiming himself to be God" (II Thessalonians 2:4). I am convinced that the world and the apostate church will believe the coming of the Antichrist to be the Second Coming of Jesus Christ, while many Jews will believe him to be their long-awaited Messiah. Even New Agers are teaching that Christ is coming again. However, the Christ they are proclaiming is not the One of the Bible, but a reincarnation of the Christ spirit.

The world will soon be offered the Antichrist, whom they'll believe to be the promised Messiah who has come to usher in a New Age, an age of peace and prosperity — the Millennium. The world will think this great charismatic leader is of God because he will appear so wonderful and powerful, and because of the miraculous manifestations he will use to deceive and unite the people and religions of the world.

What I call a "whirlwind effect" (which I witnessed with the tearing down of the Berlin Wall and the uniting of Germany) will so quickly catch the inhabitants of the earth in the excitement of this new world leader that they won't know what is really happening until it's too late. "While people are saying, 'Peace and safety,' destruction will come on them suddenly" (I Thessalonians 5:3).

Underneath the facade of the Antichrist and the False Prophet will be the stamp of the serpent whom they represent. One day that facade will be removed, but it will be too late for those who have taken the mark of the beast (Revelation 14:9-11).

The Siren Song of Unity

Excerpts from an article entitled, *The Siren Song of Unity,* by Biblical researcher Jim Weikal (whom I have worked closely with over the years) follow:

Today the world's leaders are singing an enchanting song of unification very similar to the days of Babel: "Then they said, 'Come, let us build ourselves a city, with a tower that reaches to the heavens, so that we may make a name for ourselves and not be scattered over the face of the whole earth'" (Genesis 11:4). We have a comparable message coming from the world's leaders.

The Church is subtly being directed toward Christian unity — a unity not based on the Holy Scriptures and Biblical doctrine, but founded on social issues and emotional experiences. Many pastors and believers attending ecumenical gatherings are promoting beliefs not in accord with Biblical Christianity. Pastors and other church leaders cannot blindly accept short-term benefits and not consider the long-range consequences. The long-range consequences of uniting with movements that want religious unity over Biblical unity will be compromising pastors, diminishing reliance on the Word and doctrine, lukewarm congregations, unholy alliances with any faith, and eventually embracing the religion of the Antichrist and the False Prophet.

The Bible speaks of a false world religion in the end times that is an offense to Christ. The whole Church may seem to be succumbing to the unification movement; but a remnant still exists today who have not bowed down to every new wave, new teaching, or new experience that comes along. They have not united around social issues, signs and wonders, or a lowest-common-denominator Biblical standard that any religion can join. They search the Scriptures daily, they fast, they worship, they deny themselves, they seek God's face through prayer and supplication. Their hearts are turned toward their God, asking Him what He desires. Believers like this, in fact, are united.

As the unity/ecumenical pressure increases, those opposing will be considered obstructions to a move of God. Any opposing views will be condemned as divisive, negative, proud, unloving, narrow, radical, or some other malicious label.

Don't let the current unity movement lure you away from Biblical Christianity or cause you to make a compromised commitment to the Jesus of the Bible. Instead, stand in true Biblical unity, "the faith that was once for all entrusted to the saints" (Jude 3).

Increasing Persecution

If there is going to be a new world order and a global society under the reign of Antichrist and the False Prophet, then those who will not cooperate must either be converted, silenced, or eliminated. This is exactly what Scripture indicates is going to happen.

As the current unity movement continues its influence throughout the world, those who initially indicated that they were tolerant of all religions, will become very intolerant of true believers in Jesus Christ who refuse to compromise Biblical Christianity. A day is coming when all who remain faithful to the God of the Bible will suffer persecution and possible martyrdom.

Throughout Scripture, the spirit of antichrist has always inspired persecution of God's people. It opposed Moses and Elijah. It attempted to put to death Daniel and his three friends. It killed many of the prophets of God. It encouraged the crucifixion of the Lord Jesus. It martyred Stephen (Acts 7:60), James (Acts 12:1,2), and Antipas (Revelation 2:13).

Just as Jeremiah suffered and was persecuted for speaking the true word of the Lord, so too, true believers who remain faithful will greatly suffer because of their testimony for Jesus and the Word of God. In fact, no less than five times does Revelation (in regards to the apostle John or the persecution of end-time believers who refuse to compromise) mention the utterly crucial and central importance of the Word of God and their testimony for Jesus (Revelation 1:2, 9; 6:9; 12:17; 20:4). Revelation 12:17 indicates that the Dragon (Satan) was enraged at those "who obey God's commandments and hold to the testimony of Jesus."

We are seeing an increase in opposition to Biblical Christianity. Eventually, intense persecution and martyrdom of true believers in Christ will occur worldwide, as is already occurring in many countries. Some of the reasons for the persecution and martyrdom of believers in Christ who refuse to compromise and conform follow:

1) People are being desensitized to violence. There is so much violence in the media (movies, music, cartoons, video games, etc.) that young people and adults are no longer shocked by it, but accept it as a normal way of life.

2) Biblical beliefs are being undermined, both in the secular world and by many supposed Christian leaders. They say the belief that "Jesus is the only way" is too dogmatic and old-fashioned. Their thinking is: "We all believe in the same God, so we must forget doctrinal issues and unite."

3) Biblical Christians and Jews are being labeled as the world's troublemakers. Accused of hate crimes, intolerance, and bigotry, believers in Jesus Christ will be persecuted for refusing to compromise their commitment to their Lord and Biblical Christianity.

An expert on the holocaust was asked in a television interview how such an atrocity could occur, and how so many people could quietly sit by while millions of Jews were annihilated. He responded that for years before the atrocities occurred the Jews were subtly degraded and put down through the media's propaganda, and were gradually recognized as subhuman and as troublemakers. For this reason almost everyone accepted it with little concern when the cruelties and exterminations began. This same kind of conditioning is occurring today through the media.

Love and unity are becoming the ultimate good; division is evil. Therefore, Christians who refuse to unite with the new world order — for the common good, for the salvation of our global, planetary system — are considered divisive, evil, and the real Antichrist.

Committed Christians will one day be persecuted by those professing to be the true church. Having replaced the Scriptural criteria for a true Christian with a new definition of spirituality determined by acceptance of the love and unity and the signs and wonders movements, the apostate church will oppose and seek to destroy true believers in Christ who disagree. Scripture indicates this apostate church and Antichrist system will martyr God's true believers because of their testimony for Jesus (the Jesus of the Bible, not some redefined, unbiblical Jesus) and the Word of God (Revelation 6:9; 12:17; 20:4). The False Prophet will cause all who refuse to worship the image of the Antichrist to be killed (Revelation 13:15), and the apostate church will be "drunk with the blood of the saints, the blood of those who bore testimony to Jesus" (Revelation 17:6).

Seeking Truth in the Midst of Apostasy

I have watched as many pastors and Christians have changed their beliefs and practices because of all the new teachings and phenomena sweeping the Church today. Now they do not even remotely resemble Biblical Christianity. They are becoming increasingly hostile to those who desire to stay true to the Word of God and maintain a pure testimony for Jesus. They justify it by stating that those opposed to love and unity and the new moving of the Spirit are not Christians, so it's all right to oppose them, and eventually persecute and martyr them.

The good news, however, is that in the midst of this visible apostasy, I am encountering an increasing number of believers who are genuinely hungry for true Biblical Christianity. They are earnestly seeking to know the Word of God and are being empowered by His Spirit to stand strong for the Lord and endure various trials and tribulations.

Persecution is allowed by God for the purpose of purifying His Church. Television, pornography, and the things of the world will certainly lose their appeal and seem unimportant when you, your family, and fellow believers are being persecuted or martyred. The true Church of the end times will be focused on evangelization and staying faithful to the Lord in spite of severe persecution.

Pattern of Persecution in the New Testament

We see the following pattern of persecution in the New Testament:

1) In Acts 2:47, believers were " enjoying the favor of all the people." But the tide gradually turns — Jewish leaders become disturbed at the preaching of Jesus' resurrection. They arrest Peter and John, warn them not to speak in Jesus' name, and then release them (Acts 4:1-22).

2) In Acts 5:17-42, Jewish leaders who are inflamed with jealousy over the genuine miracles and the apostles' refusal to quit preaching the resurrection of Jesus, arrest them again. This time they are flogged before they are released.

3) Then in Acts 7, Stephen is stoned and becomes the first martyr of the Church.

4) As a result of Stephen's martyrdom, an explosion of persecution occurred. Acts 8:1 says, "... On that day a great persecution broke out against the Church at Jerusalem, and all except the apostles were scattered throughout Judea and Samaria."

I believe a similar pattern of gradually increasing persecution on a global scale and then an explosion of martyrdom worldwide will occur. In the near future it will please the people and be popular to persecute the true Church, just as it was in New Testament times. They will kill you, believing they are serving God. Acts 12:1-3 states —

> It was about this time that King Herod arrested some who belonged to the church, intending to persecute them. He had James, the brother of John, put to death with the sword. When he saw that this pleased the Jews, he proceeded to seize Peter also. This happened during the Feast of Unleavened Bread.

Wearing Out the Saints

Most people during the Tribulation will choose to follow the easy and popular way of apostate Christianity. True believers, however, will suffer persecution and possibly martyrdom for being Biblical Christians who refuse to compromise their testimony for Jesus and the Word of God.

Revelation 13:7 —

> He [Antichrist] was given power to make war against the saints and to conquer them. And he was given authority over every tribe, people, language and nation.

To "make war" does not mean to wage a military campaign but refers to hostility against and destruction of God's people in whatever manner and through whatever means.

Daniel 7:21,22,25 —

> As I watched, this horn [Antichrist] was

waging war against the saints and defeating them, until the Ancient of Days came and pronounced judgment in favor of the saints of the Most High, and the time came when they possessed the kingdom. He will speak against the Most High and oppress His saints and try to change the set times and the laws. The saints will be handed over to him for a time, times and half a time.

Scripture assures us that the Lord will bring ultimate victory and that His holy people will overcome in spite of enduring such trying times during the Tribulation.

Suffering of Believers during the Tribulation

Some think that the following verses mean that believers will be raptured before the Tribulation, while others say they refer to God's wrath which we will miss, but that we will face Satan's persecution:

Revelation 3:10 —

Since you have kept My command to endure patiently, I will also keep you from the hour of trial that is going to come upon the whole world to test those who live on the earth.

I Thessalonians 1:10 —

And to wait for His Son from heaven, whom He raised from the dead — Jesus, who rescues us from the coming wrath.

No matter what your belief is concerning the timing of the rapture (pre, mid, post, or pre-wrath), Scripture clearly indicates that those who remain faithful to Christ during the Tribulation will face Satan's wrath, hunger, thirst, exposure to the elements (scorching sun), loss of home and security, persecution, torture, and even martyrdom.

Revelation 7:9-17 —

After this I looked and there before me was a great multitude that no one could count, from every nation, tribe, people and language, standing before the throne and in front of the Lamb. They were wearing white robes and were holding palm branches in their hands. And they cried out in a loud voice: "Salvation belongs to our God, who sits on the throne, and to the Lamb."

... Then one of the elders asked me, "These in white robes — who are they, and where did they come from?" I answered, "Sir, you know." And he said, "These are they who have come out of the great tribulation; they have washed their robes and made them white in the blood of the Lamb. Therefore, they are before the throne of God and serve Him day and night in His temple; and He who sits on the throne will spread His tent over them.

Never again will they hunger; never again will they thirst. The sun will not beat upon them, nor any scorching heat. For the Lamb at the center of the throne will be their Shepherd; He will lead them to springs of living water. And God will wipe away every tear from their eyes.

Revelation 6:9-11 —

When he opened the fifth seal, I saw under the altar the souls of those who had been slain because of the Word of God and the testimony they had maintained. They called out in a loud voice, "How long, Sovereign Lord, holy and true, until you judge the inhabitants of the earth and avenge our blood?" Then each of them was given a white robe, and they were told to wait a little longer, until the number of their fellow servants and brothers who were to be killed as they had been was completed.

Revelation 13:10 —

If anyone is to go into captivity, into captivity

he will go. If anyone is to be killed with the sword, with the sword he will be killed. This calls for patient endurance and faithfulness on the part of the saints.

Revelation 14:13 —

Then I heard a voice from heaven say, "Write: Blessed are the dead who die in the Lord from now on." "Yes," says the Spirit, "they will rest from their labor, for their deeds will follow them."

Revelation 16:5,6 —

Then I heard the angel in charge of the waters say: "You are just in these judgments, You who are and who were, the Holy One, because You have so judged; for they have shed the blood of Your saints and prophets, and You have given them blood to drink as they deserve."

They Overcame by the Blood of the Lamb

Believers living during the Tribulation will overcome the enemy through the blood of the Lamb and the word of their testimony. They will choose to suffer oppression, persecution, and even martyrdom rather than deny their faith in Jesus Christ. Rather than indicating Satan's triumph, the blood of the martyrs will indicate the victory of faithful followers who confirm their loyalty to Jesus by their witness even to death.

Revelation 12:11 —

They overcame him by the blood of the Lamb and by the word of their testimony; they did not love their lives so much as to shrink from death.

Revelation 20:4 —

I saw thrones on which were seated those who had been given authority to judge. And I saw the souls of those who had been beheaded because of their testimony for Jesus and because of the Word of God. They had not worshiped the beast or his image and had not received his mark on their foreheads or their hands. They came to life and reigned with Christ a thousand years.

When Jesus Christ defeats the Antichrist and the kings of the earth at Armageddon, with Him will be His called, chosen, and faithful followers (Revelation 17:14).

Apostate Church

A popular teaching today has twisted Scripture out of context to teach that an elite army of overcomers will subdue the world and destroy all the enemies of Christ. When they gain power and authority over the world, then Christ can return as they present Him the Kingdom. Many believe that a global celebration of unequalled magnitude is about to begin.

Today's "prophets" continually prophesy renewal, revival, and restoration. But is much of the revival and movement toward unity which is occurring today really a commitment to the Christ of the Bible and Biblical Christianity, or is it merely an attraction to all of the excitement and phenomena going on?

Because many so-called prophets have been prophesying for years a great revival before Christ's Second Coming, and so many pastors and Christian leaders have been repeatedly proclaiming this from their pulpits and over the radio and television, it is assumed by many that this will certainly occur, in spite of the fact that Scripture presents an entirely different end-time scenario. Scripture repeatedly warns of apostasy and deception, admonishing end-time believers to persevere, not give up, and to remain faithful to the end.

Sad indeed is the fact that New Age philosophy, which is helping to usher in what I believe will be the very religion of the Antichrist, has been adopted by many Christians today. While I do believe we are more than conquerors through Christ and we are to occupy till He comes, the teachings of many supposed believers on the last days are too close for comfort to the New Age movement and that which the Bible describes concerning the temporary regime of the Antichrist.

Scripture contradicts their theology of conquering and restoring the world before Christ returns so supposed victorious believers can present the Kingdom to Him. Those who think that we are going to Christianize the world and then Christ will come back after we have won the world had better take another look at the book of Revelation; II Thessalonians chapter 2; Daniel chapters 7, 8, 11, and 12; Matthew chapter 24; and numerous other related Scriptures.

Subjective Experiences and the Unity Movement

In these last days beware of two crucial things: 1) the false unity movement and 2) subjective experiences and phenomena that go beyond the Word of God.

We are living in a day of great deception, and Scripture strongly indicates it is going to accelerate. I am convinced that many professing Christians who are getting caught up in the unity movement, who live by the experiential, who lack discernment, and who don't rightly divide the Word of Truth, will be deceived by the great delusion Paul prophesied would overtake those who reject the love of the truth (II Thessalonians 2:10). If so many are being deceived now, how do they expect to stand when the deception gets even more difficult to discern and numerous amazing false miracles, signs, and wonders occur?

The false prophets of Jeremiah's day were prophesying peace and prosperity while Jeremiah accurately prophesied God's impending judgment because of the sin and apostasy of the people and their leaders. Then — in contrast to the false peace of the false prophets — Jeremiah prophesied the Lord's promised restoration (Jeremiah 33). I believe Scripture strongly indicates a similar end-time scenario of God's judgment on a rebellious world and apostate church (Tribulation period) and then Christ's Second Coming and promised restoration of all things. Many "Christians" who are selling out the Lord for the imitation will miss the genuine.

Is the Spirit of Judas Infiltrating the Church?

Christians should be outstanding and exemplary citizens — the "salt of the earth" and the "light of the world" — opposed to such social abuses as abortion, pornography, and the like. Christians should be involved in all aspects of society — government, law, education, health, and the arts. However, many Christians are replacing their desire to reach the world for Christ with a political and social agenda.

The heartfelt desire of Jesus for His Church is reflected in His final command to the disciples right before He ascended to heaven as recorded in Acts 1:8 —

> But you will receive power when the Holy Spirit comes on you; and you will be My witnesses in Jerusalem, and in all Judea and Samaria, and to the ends of the earth.

Instead of being trained for evangelism, Christians are being recruited to march in protests and attend rallies, and are joining forces with pseudo-Christian groups and non-Christians to implement political and social agendas. The zeal of many to win the lost is being replaced with a zeal for political activism. I am concerned that the Jesus of the Bible is being sold out and replaced by a watered-down Jesus who is tolerated by lukewarm Christians and the world — a Jesus who compromises His holiness and is less threatening to their ideologies and fits into their compromised and enforced unity.

We must be careful that the spirit of Judas does not enter the Church. It is argued that Judas betrayed Christ in order to attempt a forceful overthrow of the wicked Roman oppressors. But Jesus' purpose was clearly not to establish a physical kingdom by force at that time, but to die for the sins of the world and empower followers by His Spirit to take the Gospel to the ends of the earth (Acts 1:8). That is why Jesus and the New Testament apostles did not make politics and social activism their focal point. Today, however, many are betraying Jesus by diverting their time, money, and energy from reaching a lost world with the life-changing Gospel of Christ before His soon return, and are focusing their resources on seeking to influence their world politically and socially.

If Christians would put as much enthusiasm into personal evangelism as they do for political and social activism, and if they would spend as much time in the Word and on their knees praying for God's Spirit to empower them as they do for grasping after temporary worldly goals, imagine the eternal impact they would make around the globe. While many causes are noble, we must not permit ourselves to be hindered by any-thing that diverts or compromises the proclamation of the Gospel of Jesus Christ.

Genuine Outpouring of Spirit

While Satan pours out his spirit of deception among the Biblically illiterate, God pours out among the faithful remnant a much greater anointing of His Spirit. Those who are His own and who stay committed and true to His Word and Spirit will walk in greater discernment, wisdom, and strength than ever before.

From my research into the last days and the current trends infiltrating the Church, and from my study of God's Word and the witness of His Spirit through many hours of prayer and fasting, I am convinced that apostasy is accelerating toward its climax in total rebellion against the Lord and His Word. Evil — often disguised as good — is becoming progressively unrestrained. The Spirit of Truth is being replaced with a spirit of error.

I also believe, however, that we are on the verge of a genuine outpouring of and empowering by God's Spirit before Christ's Second Coming. Look at the 144,000 servants of God in Revelation chapter 7. Many Bible scholars believe these 144,000 from all the tribes of Israel, who have the seal of the living God (Revelation 7:2-4) and the name of the Lamb and His Father's name on their foreheads (Revelation 14:1), will be empowered by the Spirit to witness throughout the world during the Tribulation.

As we read on in Revelation chapter 7, we see "a great multitude that no one could count, from every nation, tribe, people and language, standing before the throne and in front of the Lamb" (v.9). This great multitude consists of those "who have come out of the great tribulation; they have washed their robes and made them white in the blood of the Lamb" (v.14).

We also see that the two witnesses will be supernaturally empowered to stand and be victorious until their testimony is completed (Revelation 11:3-12). Daniel 11:32 indicates that, "the people who know their God will display strength and take action" (NAS) ["shall be strong, and do exploits" – KJV]. I believe those who stay faithful to the Jesus of the Bible and the Word of God will be supernaturally empowered by His Spirit. In the midst of deception, persecution, and martyrdom, we will see the resurrection power of

Christ as manifested in the book of Acts and in the prophesies of Joel 2:28-32 — as well as an increase of the imitation and counterfeit occurring through the False Prophet and apostate church.

Belshazzar's Final Fling

Belshazzar, king of Babylon, had a "final fling" in Daniel 5. So too, the apostate church is having her "final fling." While a lost and dying world goes into eternity without Christ, an excitement-crazed church "parties in the Spirit" — drunk, laughing, falling over, dancing sensually, involving themselves in occultic techniques, and giving "new revelations" and "prophecies" that only encourage their foolish and errant ways. But the party is about to come to an end. The handwriting is on the wall.

Prophecy is being fulfilled. The new world order and the deceptive and temporary reign of the Antichrist and the False Prophet looms on the near horizon. Apostasy accelerates. Potential persecution and martyrdom for true believers in Christ draws ever closer, yet few seem to notice or care. The approaching tribulation of the Antichrist's reign of terror, God's wrath and judgment, and Christ's Second Coming are ignored or distorted by supposed believers in Christ who are too busy partying and having a "good time in the Lord" to realize the signs of the times that are being fulfilled.

Concerning the end times, Daniel 12:10 states —

Many will be purified, made spotless and refined, but the wicked will continue to be wicked. None of the wicked will understand, but those who are wise will understand.

Belshazzar, who had become preoccupied with partying and feeling good, was oblivious to what was about to happen. But Daniel knew, and so will you know of the impending events that are to come in these last days, if you spend time in the Word and get on your knees in prayer. Doing so will help you have the same discernment and ultimate victory that Daniel had.

Apostate Church Destroyed

The great prostitute (Revelation 17:1) consisting of all false religions, including apostate Christianity, will be one ecumenical universal system. The apostate church will be politically influential, materially rich, and will intoxicate the inhabitants and leaders of the world with the abominable and blasphemous teachings of her spiritual adultery (Revelation 17:1-5,15; 18:3). She will be associated with the Antichrist and use her religious power to temporarily influence him (Revelation 13:1; 17:3,7-13), as well as be responsible for the death of God's true saints (Revelation 17:6).

The name "Babylon" traces its origin to "Babel," which symbolizes false spirituality, sorcery, worldliness, and rebellion against the true God. In these last days you will either be aligned with the people and city of Babylon, thereby being drunk with the blood of the saints (Revelation 17:6), or you will be identified with the true people of God and the coming New Jerusalem by having been washed in the blood of the Lamb (Revelation 7:14).

Revelation 17:4 states —

The woman [great prostitute, apostate church] was dressed in purple and scarlet, and was glittering with gold, precious stones and pearls. She held a golden cup in her hand, filled with abominable things and the filth of her adulteries.

While the lukewarm Laodicean Church said —

"I am rich; I have acquired wealth and do not need a thing," Jesus said, "But you do not realize that you are wretched, pitiful, poor, blind and naked" (Revelation 3:17).

In spite of her confidence and sorceries, Isaiah 47:11-14 proclaimed Babylon's doom and fall —

> Disaster will come upon you, and you will not know how to conjure it away. A calamity will fall upon you that you cannot ward off with a ransom; a catastrophe you cannot foresee will suddenly come upon you. Keep on, then, with your magic spells and with your many sorceries, which you have labored at since childhood. Perhaps you will succeed, perhaps you will cause terror.
>
> All the counsel you have received has only worn you out! Let your astrologers come forward, those stargazers who make predictions month by month, let them save you from what is coming upon you. Surely they are like stubble; the fire will burn them up. They cannot even save themselves from the power of the flame ....

The Antichrist not only breaks his covenant with Israel, but he also breaks his relationship with the great prostitute, the apostate church. After using the apostate church to catapult himself into power, the Antichrist will turn on this lukewarm, backslidden church, and persecute, torture, and destroy her. This is the frightful (but just) end of an apostate church which committed spiritual adultery and intoxicated the inhabitants of the earth with the wine of her adulteries (Revelation 17:2; 18:3).

A similar lamentation will be said of the apostate church as was said about Israel by Jeremiah —

> What can I say for you? With what can I compare you, O Daughter of Jerusalem? To what can I liken you, that I may comfort you, O Virgin Daughter of Zion? Your wound is as deep as the sea. Who can heal you? The visions of your prophets were false and worthless; they did not expose your sin to ward off your captivity. The oracles they gave you were false and misleading.

All who pass your way clap their hands at you; they scoff and shake their heads at the Daughter of Jerusalem: "Is this the city that was called the perfection of beauty, the joy of the whole earth?"

All your enemies open their mouths wide against you; they scoff and gnash their teeth and say, "We have swallowed her up. This is the day we have waited for; we have lived to see it." The Lord has done what He planned; He has fulfilled His word, which He decreed long ago. He has overthrown you without pity, He has let the enemy gloat over you, He has exalted the horn of your foes (Lamentations 2:13-17).

While exiled in Babylon, Ezekiel had a vision during which God showed him the wicked and detestable things the leaders and people of Israel were doing (Ezekiel chapter 8). As a result, God stated in Ezekiel 8:18 —

Therefore I will deal with them in anger; I will not look on them with pity or spare them. Although they shout in my ears, I will not listen to them.

Today, the leaders and those who name the name of Christ are involved in the wicked and detestable practices of the world. We must heed what God told the people of Judah in Jeremiah 51:6, 7 —

Flee from Babylon! Run for your lives! Do not be destroyed because of her sins. It is time for the Lord's vengeance; He will pay her what she deserves. Babylon was a gold cup in the Lord's hand; she made the whole earth drunk. The nations drank her wine; therefore they have now gone mad.

In similar fashion, Revelation 18:4 gives God's prophetic call to the last generation of believers to separate from the world and false religion. It says —

Then I heard another voice from heaven say: "Come out of her, my people, so that you will not share in her sins, so that you will not receive any of her plagues."

Revelation 14:8 proclaims —

A second angel followed and said, "Fallen! Fallen is Babylon the Great, which made all the nations drink the maddening wine of her adulteries."

Revelation 19:2 indicates that God has —

... condemned the great prostitute who corrupted the earth by her adulteries. He has avenged on her the blood of His servants.

Scripture gives the tragic end of the once wealthy, powerful, and unified apostate church. Her demise probably occurs after the Antichrist desecrates the Temple and proclaims himself to be God. Desiring only himself to be worshiped, he will seek to destroy anything that even remotely resembles Christianity.

Revelation 17:1 states —

One of the seven angels who had the seven bowls came and said to me, "Come, I will show you the punishment of the great prostitute, who sits on many waters."

Revelation 17:16,17 gives additional insight —

The beast [Antichrist] and the ten horns [ten kings – Revelation 17:12] you saw will hate the prostitute. They will bring her to ruin and leave her naked; they will eat her flesh and burn her with fire. For God has put it into their hearts to accomplish His purpose by agreeing to give the beast their power to rule, until God's words are fulfilled.

Leviticus 21:9 —

If a priest's daughter defiles herself by becoming a prostitute, she disgraces her father; she must be burned in the fire.

Just as the daughter of a priest was burned with fire for prostitution, likewise, the spiritual prostitute who infects and influences the world with her sorceries will be burned with fire (Revelation 17:16; 18:8, 9).

The apostate church in harmony with the rebellious, occultic system of Babylon will be judged severely and destroyed quickly. God will judge Babylon the Great for the way she treated His saints. Revelation 18:20 states —

Rejoice over her, O heaven! Rejoice, saints and apostles and prophets! God has judged her for the way she treated you.

Furthermore, the Antichrist, False Prophet, and the kings of the earth and their armies will meet their demise at Armageddon by Christ at His Second Coming (Revelation 16:14,16; 17:12-14; 19:11-21).

In contrast to God's judgment on an apostate church and a rebellious world, Christ's true bride — those committed to the testimony of the Jesus of the Bible and obedient to the Word of God — will rejoice and be glad when the wedding supper of the Lamb has come (Revelation 19:7).

True believers in Christ will rule and reign with Him during the Millennium and throughout eternity (Revelation 2:26; 3:21; 5:10; 20:4, 6; 22:5). The faithful will inherit all God has prepared for those who overcome (Revelation 21:7).

Awesomeness of God Displayed in Judgment

The God of the Bible is a loving and patient God, but He is also a God of justice who does not tolerate sin and rebellion. Scripture repeatedly indicates that though He is gracious and merciful, He will not hold back His hand of devastating judgment forever. Sooner or later He acts against sin and rebellion, against those who fight against His holiness and His holy people.

II Thessalonians 1:6-10 —

God is just: He will pay back trouble to those who trouble you and give relief to you who are troubled, and to us as well. This will happen when the Lord Jesus is revealed from heaven in blazing fire with His powerful angels. He will punish those who do not know God and do not obey the Gospel of our Lord Jesus. They will be punished with everlasting destruction and shut out from the presence of the Lord and from the majesty of His power on the day He comes to be glorified in His holy people and to be marveled at among all those who have believed. This includes you, because you believed our testimony to you.

Isaiah 2:17-22 —

The arrogance of man will be brought low and the pride of men humbled; the Lord alone will be exalted in that day, and the idols will totally disappear. Men will flee to caves in the rocks and to holes in the ground from dread of the Lord and the splendor of His majesty, when He rises to shake the earth. In that day men will throw away to the rodents and bats their idols of silver and idols of gold, which they made to worship. They will flee to caverns in the rocks and to the overhanging crags from dread of the Lord and the splendor of His majesty, when He rises to shake the earth. Stop trusting in man, who has but a breath in his nostrils. Of what account is he?

Isaiah 13:6-13 —

Wail, for the day of the Lord is near; it will come like destruction from the Almighty. Because of this, all hands will go limp, every man's heart will melt. Terror will seize them, pain and anguish will grip them; they will writhe like a woman in labor. They will look aghast at each other, their faces aflame. See, the day of the Lord is coming — a cruel day, with wrath and fierce anger — to make the land desolate and destroy the sinners within it.

The stars of heaven and their constellations will not show their light. The rising sun will be darkened and the moon will not give its light. I will punish the world for its evil, the wicked for their sins. I will put an end to the arrogance of the haughty and will humble the pride of the ruthless. I will make man scarcer than pure gold, more rare than the gold of Ophir. Therefore I will make the heavens tremble; and the earth will shake from its place at the wrath of the Lord Almighty, in the day of His burning anger.

Isaiah 24:1,19-23 —

See, the Lord is going to lay waste the earth

and devastate it; He will ruin its face and scatter its inhabitants. The earth is broken up, the earth is split asunder, the earth is thoroughly shaken. The earth reels like a drunkard, it sways like a hut in the wind; so heavy upon it is the guilt of its rebellion that it falls — never to rise again.

In that day the Lord will punish the powers in the heavens above and the kings on the earth below. They will be herded together like prisoners bound in a dungeon; they will be shut up in prison and be punished after many days. The moon will be abashed, the sun ashamed; for the Lord Almighty will reign on Mount Zion and in Jerusalem, and before its elders, gloriously.

Jeremiah 25:29-33 —

See, I am beginning to bring disaster on the city that bears my Name, and will you indeed go unpunished? You will not go unpunished, for I am calling down a sword upon all who live on the earth, declares the Lord Almighty.

Now prophesy all these words against them and say to them: "The Lord will roar from on high; He will thunder from His holy dwelling and roar mightily against His land. He will shout like those who tread the grapes, shout against all who live on the earth. The tumult will resound to the ends of the earth, for the Lord will bring charges against the nations; He will bring judgment on all mankind and put the wicked to the sword," declares the Lord.

This is what the Lord Almighty says: "Look! Disaster is spreading from nation to nation; a mighty storm is rising from the ends of the earth." At that time those slain by the Lord will be everywhere — from one end of the earth to the other. They will not be mourned or gathered up or buried, but will be like refuse lying on the ground."

Ezekiel 39:7,8 —

I will make known My holy name among My people Israel. I will no longer let My holy name be profaned, and the nations will know that I the Lord am the Holy One in Israel. It is coming! It will surely take place, declares the Sovereign Lord. This is the day I have spoken of.

Ezekiel 39:17-22 —

Son of man, this is what the Sovereign Lord says: Call out to every kind of bird and all the wild animals: "Assemble and come together from all around to the sacrifice I am preparing for you, the great sacrifice on the mountains of Israel. There you will eat flesh and drink blood. You will eat the flesh of mighty men and drink the blood of the princes of the earth as if they were rams and lambs, goats and bulls — all of them fattened animals from Bashan. At the sacrifice I am preparing for you, you will eat fat till you are glutted and drink blood till you are drunk. At My table you will eat your fill of horses and riders, mighty men and soldiers of every kind," declares the Sovereign Lord.

I will display My glory among the nations, and all the nations will see the punishment I inflict and the hand I lay upon them. From that day forward the house of Israel will know that I am the Lord their God.

Joel 2:1-31 —

Blow the trumpet in Zion; sound the alarm on My holy hill. Let all who live in the land tremble, for the day of the Lord is coming. It is close at hand — a day of darkness and gloom, a day of clouds and blackness. Like dawn spreading across the mountains a large and mighty army comes, such as never was of old nor ever will be in ages to come. ...

Before them the earth shakes, the sky trembles, the sun and moon are darkened, and the stars no longer shine. The Lord thunders at the head of His army; His forces are beyond number, and mighty are those who obey His command. The day of the Lord is great; it is dreadful. Who can endure it? ...

I will show wonders in the heavens and on the earth, blood and fire and billows of smoke. The sun will be turned to darkness and the moon to blood before the coming of the great and dreadful day of the Lord.

Joel 3:14-16 —

Multitudes, multitudes in the valley of decision! For the day of the Lord is near in the valley of decision. The sun and moon will be darkened, and the stars no longer shine. The Lord will roar from Zion and thunder from Jerusalem; the earth and the sky will tremble. But the Lord will be a refuge for His people, a stronghold for the people of Israel.

Matthew 24:29 —

Immediately after the distress of those days "the sun will be darkened, and the moon will not give its light; the stars will fall from the sky, and the heavenly bodies will be shaken."

Revelation 6:12-17 —

I watched as He opened the sixth seal. There was a great earthquake. The sun turned black like sackcloth made of goat hair, the whole moon turned blood red, and the stars in the sky fell to earth, as late figs drop from a fig tree when shaken by a strong wind. The sky receded like a scroll, rolling up, and every mountain and island was removed from its place. Then the kings of the earth, the princes, the generals, the rich, the mighty, and every slave and every free man hid in caves and among the rocks of the mountains. They called to the mountains and the rocks, "Fall on us and hide us from the face of Him who sits on the throne and from the wrath of the Lamb! For the great day of their wrath has come, and who can stand?"

Revelation 16:17-21 —

The seventh angel poured out his bowl into the air, and out of the temple came a loud voice from the throne, saying, "It is done!" Then there came flashes of lightning, rumblings, peals of thunder and a severe earthquake. No earthquake like it has ever occurred since man has been on earth, so tremendous was the quake. The great city split into three parts, and the cities of the nations collapsed. God remembered Babylon the Great and gave her the cup filled with the wine of the fury of His wrath. Every island fled away and the mountains could not be found. From the sky huge hailstones of about a hundred pounds each fell upon men. And they cursed God on account of the plague of hail, because the plague was so terrible.

Revelation 18:5-8, 21 —

For her [Babylon the Great] sins are piled up to heaven, and God has remembered her crimes. Give back to her as she has given; pay her back double for what she has done. Mix her a double portion from her own cup. Give her as much torture and grief as the glory and luxury she gave herself. In her heart she boasts, "I sit as queen; I am not a widow, and I will never mourn." Therefore in one day her plagues will overtake her: death, mourning and famine. She will be consumed by fire, for mighty is the Lord God who judges her.

Then a mighty angel picked up a boulder the size of a large millstone and threw it into the sea, and said: "With such violence the great city of Babylon will be thrown down, never to be found again.

Revelation 19:11 —

I saw heaven standing open and there before

me was a white horse, whose rider is called Faithful and True. With justice He judges and makes war.

Revelation 19:17-21 —

And I saw an angel standing in the sun, who cried in a loud voice to all the birds flying in midair, "Come, gather together for the great supper of God, so that you may eat the flesh of kings, generals, and mighty men, of horses and their riders, and the flesh of all people, free and slave, small and great."

Then I saw the beast and the kings of the earth and their armies gathered together to make war against the Rider on the horse and His army. But the beast was captured, and with him the false prophet who had performed the miraculous signs on his behalf. With these signs he had deluded those who had received the mark of the beast and worshiped his image. The two of them were thrown alive into the fiery lake of burning sulfur. The rest of them were killed with the sword that came out of the mouth of the Rider on the horse, and all the birds gorged themselves on their flesh.

The Lord will not restrain His righteous judgment much longer. His delay in fulfilling His prophetic Word is nearing an end.

Defeat of Antichrist

While ministering in Germany, I had a chance to visit Nuremberg where Hitler's rallies began and where the trials of many of the Nazi leaders were held. It is of interest to point out some of the similarities of Hitler's and the Antichrist's regimes.

• Just as a nation joined Hitler in his treachery and deception because he seemed to be their savior — and unstoppable — the world will join the Antichrist's reign of treachery and deception because he will appear to be an unstoppable savior.

Revelation 13:4 —

Men worshiped the dragon because he had given authority to the beast, and they also worshiped the beast and asked, "Who is like the beast? Who can make war against him?"

• However, just as Hitler's regime came to an end and justice was meted out, the end of the Antichrist's regime also will come and justice will be meted out.

• Hitler's henchmen were tried by an international tribunal, but the Antichrist's fate is already sealed and the world will be tried by God Himself at the Great White Throne judgment (Revelation 20:11-15).

• Hitler's henchmen were brave and bold when in power, but they were not so when captured and tried. Likewise, Antichrist and his associates will be arrogant and blaspheme God (Revelation 13:6; Daniel 11:36; II Thessalonians 2:3,4), but they will cower in fear before the Lord when their judgment comes.

• Most of Hitler's henchmen who were tried were executed (a few committed suicide). They were shown lying dead and helpless. Their bodies were cremated and their ashes were dispersed to the winds. Antichrist and those who follow him will also be helpless and banned from God's presence forever.

• Hitler's henchmen enjoyed wild parties and lived in opulence and pleasure while those they oppressed were deprived, starved, and tortured. Those who follow Antichrist will think they have a destiny of opulence and pleasure, but Scripture indicates it will be short-lived. History will repeat itself in that: "Those who once ate delicacies are destitute in the streets. Those nurtured in purple now lie on ash heaps" (Lamentations 4:5). The eternal destiny of Antichrist and his followers is the lake of fire (Revelation 14:9,10; 19:20; 20:14,15). But God's promise to true believers is: "In Thy presence is fullness of joy; at Thy right hand there are pleasures for evermore" (Psalm 16:11 - kjv).

The Darkest Hour

The reign of Antichrist is expected to be the dawning of a golden era of peace, prosperity, and unity. Actually, it will become the darkest hour earth will ever know.

Near the end of the seven years the Antichrist and the kings of the earth and their armies will gather together to fight against the Lord at Armageddon (Megiddo, overlooking the valley of Jezreel in northern Israel).

Revelation 16:13 -16 states —

Then I saw three evil spirits that looked like frogs; they came out of the mouth of the dragon, out of the mouth of the beast and out of the mouth of the false prophet. They are spirits of demons performing miraculous signs, and they go out to the kings of the whole world, to gather them for the battle on the great day of God Almighty. "Behold, I come like a thief! Blessed is he who stays awake and keeps his clothes with him, so that he may not go naked and be shamefully exposed." Then they gathered the kings together to the place that in Hebrew is called Armageddon.

Revelation 19:19,20 says —

And I saw the beast and the kings of the earth and their armies, assembled to make war against Him who sat upon the horse, and against His army. And the beast was seized, and with him the false prophet who performed the signs in his presence, by which he deceived those who had received the mark of the beast and those who worshiped his image; these two were thrown alive into the lake of fire which burns with brimstone (NAS).

II Thessalonians 2:8 —

And then the lawless one will be revealed, whom the Lord Jesus will overthrow with the breath of His mouth and destroy by the splendor of His coming.

Revelation 19:15,16 —

Out of His mouth comes a sharp sword with which to strike down the nations. "He will rule them with an iron scepter." He treads the winepress of the fury of the wrath of God Almighty. On His robe and on His thigh He has this name written: KING OF KINGS AND LORD OF LORDS.

The Jesus of the Bible Will Return

The time is coming when the kingdom of this world will become the Kingdom of our Lord (Revelation 11:15). He will establish His righteous Kingdom wherein true believers will rule and reign with Him for eternity and inherit all God has prepared for us.

Some generation is going to see the fulfillment of Revelation and all the Biblical prophecies concerning Christ's return. I am convinced we are that generation. There's no doubt about it — Jesus is coming back, but not as a servant like He did the first time. He is returning in all His glory as the King of kings and Lord of lords.

Revelation 1:14-17 says concerning the glorified Christ —

His head and hair were white like wool, as white as snow, and His eyes were like blazing fire. His feet were like bronze glowing in a furnace, and His voice was like the sound of rushing waters. In His right hand He held seven stars, and out of His mouth came a sharp double-edged sword. His face was like the sun shining in all its brilliance. When I saw Him, I fell at His feet as though dead. Then He placed His right hand on me and said: "Do not be afraid. I am the First and the Last."

You may wonder just how we can know when the true Christ returns. According to Scripture, no one will have to wonder at the Second Coming of Jesus Christ. Revelation 1:7 says —

Look, He is coming with the clouds, and every eye will see Him, even those who pierced Him; and all the peoples of the earth will mourn because of Him. So shall it be! Amen.

In Acts 1:11, as Jesus ascended to heaven, two angels said to the disciples —

Men of Galilee, why do you stand here looking into the sky? This same Jesus, who has been taken from you into heaven, will come back in the same way you have seen Him go into heaven.

Matthew 24:27-31 says —

For as lightning that comes from the east is visible even in the west, so will be the coming of the Son of Man. ... At that time the sign of the Son of Man will appear in the sky, and all the nations of the earth will mourn. They will see the Son of Man coming on the clouds of the sky, with power and great glory. And He will send His angels with a loud trumpet call, and they will gather His elect from the four winds, from one end of the heavens to the other.

Daniel 7:13,14 says —

In my vision at night I looked, and there before me was one like a Son of Man, coming with the clouds of heaven. He approached the Ancient of Days and was led into His presence. He was given authority, glory and sovereign power; all peoples, nations and men of every language worshiped Him. His dominion is an everlasting dominion that will not pass away, and His kingdom is one that will never be destroyed.

We Will Be Transformed

I Corinthians 15:51,52 reveals that when Christ returns believers will be transformed. It says —

Listen, I tell you a mystery: We will not all sleep, but we will all be changed — in a flash, in the twinkling of an eye, at the last trumpet. For the trumpet will sound, the dead will be raised imperishable, and we will be changed.

I Thessalonians 4:16-18 states —

For the Lord Himself will come down from heaven, with a loud command, with the voice of the archangel and with the trumpet call of God, and the dead in Christ will rise first. After that, we who are still alive and are left will be caught up together with them in the clouds to meet the Lord in the air. And so we will be with the Lord forever. Therefore encourage each other with these words.

At His Second Coming, the Biblical evidence, cataclysmic signs, and physical transformation of believers will undeniably confirm Him to be the true Messiah.

Lift Up Your Heads

Shortly before Desert Storm, I spoke at a military base on the topic of *The Last Days.* I told the officers and enlisted men and their families, "We know something big is about to come down because of all the signs and indicating factors and the continued buildup of U.S. and Allied troops." A few months later in January of 1991, "something big" did happen — the U.S. and the Allies declared war and attacked Iraq.

We know that "something big" is about to happen prophetically because we see all the "buildup" and "signs of the times" being fulfilled regarding the Lord's return.

Birth Pains

Jesus stated in Matthew 24:4-8 —

Watch out that no one deceives you. For many will come in My name, claiming, "I am the Christ," and will deceive many. You will hear of wars and rumors of wars, but see to it that you are not alarmed. Such things must happen, but the end is still to come. Nation will rise against nation, and kingdom against kingdom. There will be famines and earth-quakes in various places. All these are the beginning of birth pains.

Jesus compared the signs of His return with a woman going through birth pains (Matthew 24:8). The closer she gets to delivery, the more frequent and intense are her contractions and pain — until finally the child is born. Likewise, the more frequent and intense the indicating signs become, the closer we are to the Lord's Second Coming.

I am not saying it's going to happen today or this week or even this year or next, but I am convinced that we are the generation and this is the season when prophetic Scripture and the book of Revelation will be fulfilled. I have not come to this conclusion quickly. After spending much time over a period of many years in prayer, fasting, and prophetic research, I am convinced that you and I will see the culmination — we're seeing the beginning stages now, but we will witness the ultimate fulfillment of what Jesus Christ and the Biblical prophets foretold.

When Will You Believe?

Prophecies have at times been misunderstood by the Jews and the Church. The Jews didn't see all of the Messianic prophecies attained (such as global peace) so they rejected Jesus Christ as the Messiah. They did not understand that the remaining prophecies in the Hebrew Bible would be fulfilled at His Second Coming.

In similar fashion, when the Second Coming of Christ was delayed, many in the Church concluded the remaining prophecies were merely to be spiritually achieved or were already attained. However, just as Jesus Christ fulfilled numerous precise Messianic prophecies during His first coming, He will likewise complete the remaining ones at His Second Coming.

Amazing prophecies written thousands of years ago are coming about or have the potential in the very near future to be accomplished. How many specific prophecies have to occur before the Jews will admit that the New Testament is divinely inspired and Jesus of Nazareth is the Messiah? How many prophecies have to happen before the Church acknowledges that Jesus Christ is returning soon, and Revelation is about to be consummated?

When the Temple is rebuilt on the Temple Mount in Jerusalem, then will you believe? Or how about when there is a global society with a one-world monetary system, government, and religion? Perhaps, when a seven-year peace treaty is signed with Israel you will believe? Maybe it will take a cashless society with the inability to buy or sell without a mark on your hand or forehead to open your eyes? When the image of the Antichrist is worshiped by the inhabitants of the earth, then will you believe? When the two witnesses will be seen lying in the street of Jerusalem for three-and-a-half days? Or maybe when Jerusalem is surrounded by hostile nations? What about when the actual battle of Armageddon occurs and Christ returns in all His glory, will you then finally believe?

I stayed at the house of a prominent scientist while doing ministry in New York City. During a discussion on Bible prophecy and the book of Revelation, he said to me, "Five years ago I thought anyone who believed in the book of Revelation was crazy, but now I am convinced that in our lifetime Revelation will be fulfilled." I concur with him wholeheartedly.

Come, Lord Jesus

A correct view of Biblical prophecy and anticipation of Christ's soon return will restore your hope, joy, and zeal for evangelism, and motivate you to live a holy life.

Those of us who are ready for His appearing are saying, "Come, Lord Jesus" (Revelation 22:20). We do not have to be afraid or intimidated by what is coming on the world scene. As believers in Christ we are more than conquerors. We are overcomers through Him. We will be empowered to occupy until He comes and be victorious — even in the face of death — by the blood of the Lamb and the Word of God.

I am not distressed or depressed — I am excited. I am not worried or discouraged — I am encouraged. I am not terrified or fearful — I am confident in the Lord. We are living during the most exciting time in the history of the world. All the prophets looked forward to the time when God will fulfill all of His promises.

Jesus said —

When these things begin to take place, stand up and lift up your heads, because your redemption is drawing near (Luke 21:28).

God Has it All under Control

I have read the book of Revelation through many times, and one truth stands out very strongly — God has it all under control. Satan, the Antichrist, the False Prophet, the new world order, the apostate church, all of nature — everything is under God's control. God is the One who is orchestrating these things to accomplish His purpose for the ages.

I understand only to a limited degree why God is allowing all this to happen, but I know that when it is all over true believers will say, "True and just are His judgments" (Revelation 19:2; also 16:5-7 and 15:3).

The following are a few of the many Scriptures in Revelation which indicate that God is the One who is in control of all that will happen:

Revelation 7: 2,3 —

Then I saw another angel coming up from the east, having the seal of the living God. He called out in a loud voice to the four angels who had been given power to harm the land and the sea: "Do not harm the land or the sea or the trees until we put a seal on the foreheads of the servants of our God."

Revelation 9:4,5 —

They were told not to harm the grass of the earth or any plant or tree, but only those people who did not have the seal of God on their foreheads. They were not given power to kill them, but only to torture them for five months. And the agony they suffered was like that of the sting of a scorpion when it strikes a man.

Revelation 11:3,7 —

And I will give power to My two witnesses, and they will prophesy for 1,260 days, clothed in sackcloth. Now when they have finished their testimony, the beast that comes up from the Abyss will attack them, and overpower and kill them.

Revelation 16:9 -11 —

They were seared by the intense heat and they cursed the name of God, who had control over these plagues, but they refused to repent and glorify Him. The fifth angel poured out his bowl on the throne of the beast, and his kingdom was plunged into darkness. Men gnawed their tongues in agony and cursed the God of heaven because of their pains and their sores, but they refused to repent of what they had done.

Revelation 17:14 —

They will make war against the Lamb, but the Lamb will overcome them because He is Lord of lords and King of kings — and with Him will be His called, chosen and faithful followers.

Revelation 17:17 —

For God has put it into their hearts to accomplish His purpose by agreeing to give the beast their power to rule, until God's words are fulfilled.

The Great White Throne Judgment

Following the Tribulation and the battle of Armageddon, Satan will be bound in the bottomless pit for a thousand years (Revelation 20:1-3), during which time believers will reign with Christ (Revelation 20:4,6). After the Millennium of Christ's rule on earth in righteousness, peace, and joy, Satan is released from the bottomless pit for a short season (Revelation 20:3,7). He deceives the nations one last time (Revelation 20:8,9) and is then thrown into the lake of fire for eternity (Revelation 20:10). The Great White Throne judgment follows (Revelation 20:11-15).

Every person who did not have part in the first resurrection will be resurrected to stand before the Great White Throne judgment. Earth and sky will flee from the presence of the One who is seated on the throne removing any possible place to hide. From its final eternal verdict there will be no appeal. Anyone whose name is not written in the book of life will be thrown into the lake of fire.

Revelation 20:11-15 —

Then I saw a great white throne and Him who was seated on it. Earth and sky fled from His presence, and there was no place for them.

And I saw the dead, great and small, standing before the throne, and books were opened. Another book was opened, which is the book of life. The dead were judged according to what they had done as recorded in the books.

The sea gave up the dead that were in it, and death and Hades gave up the dead that were in them, and each person was judged according to what he had done.

Then death and Hades were thrown into the lake of fire. The lake of fire is the second death. If anyone's name was not found written in the book of life, he was thrown into the lake of fire.

We are told in Revelation 21:1 what happens following the Great White Throne judgment —

Then I saw a new heaven and a new earth, for the first heaven and the first earth had passed away, and there was no longer any sea.

Isaiah 65:17,18 —

Behold, I will create new heavens and a new earth. The former things will not be remembered, nor will they come to mind. But be glad and rejoice forever in what I will create, for I will create Jerusalem to be a delight and its people a joy.

Paradise Restored

In Genesis, fallen man and woman are banished from the Garden of Eden and the tree of life (3:22-24). In Revelation, redeemed men and women receive the New Jerusalem (21:1,2,10-27) and are given access to the tree of life (22:2).

In Genesis, death and suffering enter (3:16-19). In Revelation, God wipes every tear from the eyes of His children and removes death, mourning, crying, and pain (21:4).

In Genesis, disobedient Adam and Eve hid from the Lord God (3:8). In Revelation, believers live with God (21:3) and see His face (22:4). We will be in Christ's presence beholding His glory throughout all eternity.

Matthew 5:8 —

Blessed are the pure in heart, for they will see God.

I Corinthians 13:12 —

Now we see but a poor reflection as in a mirror; then we shall see face to face. Now I know in part; then I shall know fully, even as I am fully known.

I John 3:2 —

> Dear friends, now we are children of God, and what we will be has not yet been made known. But we know that when He appears, we shall be like Him, for we shall see Him as He is.

Truly, the Lord is faithful! All the promises and prophecies throughout Scripture dovetail into fulfillment in the last few chapters of Revelation.

The Holy City, the New Jerusalem, comes down out of heaven from God, prepared as a bride beautifully dressed for her husband (Revelation 21:2, 9-21). The following describes the eternal home of true believers in Christ:

• The dwelling of God will be with men, and He will live with us. We will be His people, and God Himself will be with us and be our God (Revelation 21:3).

• He will wipe every tear from our eyes. There will be no more death or mourning or crying or pain (Revelation 21:4).

• Those who overcome will inherit the New Jerusalem (Revelation 21:7).

• The New Jerusalem will shine with the glory of God, and its brilliance will be like that of a precious jewel (Revelation 21:11).

• There is no Temple in the New Jerusalem, because the Lord God Almighty and the Lamb shall be its Temple (Revelation 21:22).

• The Holy City does not need the sun or the moon to shine on it, for the glory of God gives it light, and the Lamb is its lamp (Revelation 21:23).

• The nations will walk by its light, and the kings of the earth will bring their splendor into it (Revelation 21:24,26).

• Its gates will never be shut, for there is no night there (Revelation 21:25; 22:5).

• Nothing unclean and no one who practices abomination and lying shall ever come into it (Revelation 21:27).

• The river of the water of life, as clear as crystal, will flow from the throne of God and of the Lamb down the middle of the great street of the Holy City (Revelation 22:1,2).

• On each side of the river will stand the tree of life (Revelation 22:2). The tree of life once guarded by the cherubim with the flaming sword at Eden is now freely available. No longer will there be any curse (Revelation 22:3).

• The throne of God and of the Lamb will be in the New Jerusalem (Revelation 22:3).

• We will see His face, and His name will be on our foreheads (Revelation 22:4).

• We will reign with Him forever and ever (Revelation 22:5).

Nothing Impure to Enter God's Holy City

Revelation 21:8 states —

But the cowardly, the unbelieving, the vile, the murderers, the sexually immoral, those who practice magic arts, the idolaters and all liars — their place will be in the fiery lake of burning sulfur. This is the second death.

Revelation 21:27 reveals that nothing impure nor anyone who does what is shameful or deceitful will enter God's Holy City, but only those whose names are written in the Lamb's book of life.

Revelation 22:15 likewise makes known that practitioners of magic arts, the sexually immoral, murderers, idolaters, and everyone who loves and practices falsehood will not be allowed to enter God's eternal Kingdom.

In contrast, Revelation 22:14 promises —

Blessed are those who wash their robes, that they may have the right to the tree of life and may go through the gates into the city.

God has prepared the New Jerusalem for true believers in Christ. We will have all eternity to enjoy His bountiful blessings. If we have been faithful over small things in this life, He will make us ruler over much in the next. We who have been redeemed by Christ, whose names are written in the Lamb's book of life, will enter the New Jerusalem to rule and reign with Christ for eternity and receive everything He has prepared for us.

How refreshing are the words of Revelation 22:17 —

The Spirit and the bride say, "Come!" And let him who hears say, "Come!" Whoever is thirsty, let him come; and whoever wishes, let him take the free gift of the water of life.

Closing Challenge

The three main rebukes the resurrected Christ gave when addressing the seven churches in Revelation chapters 2 and 3 were for: 1) leaving their first love — being lukewarm; 2) involvement in sexual immorality; and 3) tolerating false teaching.

The three main commendations the resurrected Christ gave the churches were for their: 1) love and faith; 2) endurance and perseverance; and 3) adherence to sound doctrine and avoidance of false teaching.

The Church today must consider the eternal implications of His rebukes and commendations and live accordingly. Be aware of any deception, idolatry, and disloyalty to Jesus that is evident in your life. Replace it with the truth of God's Word, His lordship, and an undying loyalty to Jesus.

A Word to Both Bereans and Those in the "New Movement of the Holy Spirit"

To those who are Biblical researchers and Berean Christians, I believe the letter to the Church in Ephesus (Revelation 2:1-7) is relevant for you. The Lord knows your deeds, hard work, and perseverance. He knows you cannot tolerate wicked men, that you have tested those who claim to be apostles but are not, and have found them false. You have persevered and have endured many hardships for His name, and have not grown weary. Yet, He cautions you to evaluate: Have you forsaken your first love? If so, remember the height from which you have fallen. Repent and do the things you did at first. If you do not repent, He will come to you and remove your lamp stand (church or ministry).

Don't allow your zeal for the truth to cause you to lose your love and desire for Jesus Christ Himself. Seek Him with all your heart through prayer and fasting, as well as studying His Word. Proclaim, with undying love, His salvation to a lost and searching world.

To those who are embracing the "new movement of the Holy Spirit," I believe the letters to the churches in Pergamum (Revelation 2:12-17) and Thyatira (Revelation 2:18-29) are relevant for you. He sees how you strive to remain true to His name and do not renounce your faith in Him. He sees your deeds, your love and faith, your service and perseverance, and that you are now doing more than you did at first.

Nevertheless, He has this against you: You hold to the teachings of Balaam who taught Balak to entice the Israelites to sin by eating food sacrificed to idols and by committing sexual immorality. Likewise you hold to the teachings of the Nicolaitans. Repent therefore! Otherwise, He will soon come to you and will fight against you with the sword of His mouth (the Word of God). And you tolerate that woman Jezebel, who calls herself a prophetess. By her teaching, she misleads His servants into sexual immorality and eating of food sacrificed to idols. He will make those who commit adultery with her to eventually suffer intensely, unless they repent of their ways.

Don't allow compromise or a desire for unity and signs and wonders to cause you to engage in beliefs and phenomena which will lead into spiritual adultery and idolatry.

Watchfulness

Every believer is responsible to be ready, alert, and watchful for the Lord's return. Jesus stated in Luke 12:35-40 —

> Be dressed ready for service and keep your lamps burning, like men waiting for their master to return from a wedding banquet, so that when he comes and knocks they can immediately open the door for him. It will be good for those servants whose master finds them watching when he comes. I tell you the truth, he will dress himself to serve, will have them recline at the table and will come and wait on them. It will be good for those servants whose master finds them ready, even if he comes in the second or third watch of the night. But understand this: If the owner of the house had known at what hour the thief was coming, he would not have let his house be broken into. You also must be ready, because the Son of Man will come at an hour when you do not expect Him.

Jesus used the following parable in Luke 12:42-46 to illustrate the blessings the watchful and faithful steward will receive and the punishment meted out to the indifferent and unfaithful steward —

> The Lord answered, "Who then is the faithful and wise manager, whom the master puts in charge of his servants to give them their food allowance at the proper time? It will be good for that servant whom the master finds doing so when he returns. I tell you the truth, he will put him in charge of all his possessions. But suppose the servant says to

himself, 'My master is taking a long time in coming,' and he then begins to beat the menservants and maidservants and to eat and drink and get drunk. The master of that servant will come on a day when he does not expect him and at an hour he is not aware of. He will cut him to pieces and assign him a place with the unbelievers."

The ongoing prayer of my ministry is:

"Lord, use me to turn the hearts of Your people back to You, or let me die trying. Help me to motivate them to walk in endurance and faithfulness until You return."

Endurance during Last Days

Jesus asked in Luke 18:8, "When the Son of Man comes, will He find faith on the earth?" The sad reality is that in the case of many supposed Christians the answer will be, "No." Yet for true believers in Christ who know His Word and are empowered by His Spirit to walk in endurance and faithfulness, the answer will be an emphatic, "Yes!"

One of the most important admonitions Jesus gave — repeated over and over in Revelation and in many other Scriptures — concerns His imminent return and His exhortation to endure, remain faithful, hold on, overcome, persevere, and stand firm to the end.

Matthew 10:21,22 —

Brother will betray brother to death, and a father his child; children will rebel against their parents and have them put to death. All men will hate you because of Me, but he who stands firm to the end will be saved.

Matthew 24:12-14 —

Because of the increase of wickedness, the love of most will grow cold, but he who stands firm to the end will be saved. And this gospel of the kingdom will be preached in the whole world as a testimony to all nations, and then the end will come.

Luke 21:16-19 —

You will be betrayed even by parents, brothers, relatives and friends, and they will put some of you to death. All men will hate you because of Me. But not a hair of your head will perish. By standing firm you will gain life.

James 5:7,8 —

Be patient, then, brothers, until the Lord's coming. See how the farmer waits for the land to yield its valuable crop and how patient he is for the autumn and spring rains. You too, be patient and stand firm, because the Lord's coming is near.

Revelation 2:10 —

Do not be afraid of what you are about to suffer. I tell you, the devil will put some of you in prison to test you, and you will suffer persecution for ten days. Be faithful, even to the point of death, and I will give you the crown of life.

Revelation 2:25,26 —

Only hold on to what you have until I come. To him who overcomes and does My will to the end, I will give authority over the nations.

Revelation 13:9,10 —

He who has an ear, let him hear. If anyone is to go into captivity, into captivity he will go. If anyone is to be killed with the sword, with the sword he will be killed. This calls for patient endurance and faithfulness on the part of the saints.

Revelation 14:12 —

This calls for patient endurance on the part of the saints who obey God's commandments and remain faithful to Jesus.

Revelation 21:7 —

He who overcomes will inherit all this, and I will be his God and he will be My son.

Two Types of Christians

As I travel and minister throughout the world, I am encountering two types of Christians. First, I see those who are involving themselves in the cares of the world and the lusts of the flesh. They are lukewarm and not wholeheartedly committed to the Lord. Being disobedient and undisciplined, they fill their bodies, minds, and spirits with garbage. Having a spirit of compromise and cowardice, they are conformers instead of overcomers. They are involved in fleshly and demonic phenomena attributed to the Holy Spirit. In the guise of love and unity they are compromised in unholy alliances. They lack discernment and do not recognize the signs of the times. They spend little (if any) time reading the Scriptures. They do not get on their knees in prayer and fast to seek the Lord and His will with all their hearts. They have drifted from Biblical Christianity. Unless they repent, they will become part of the apostasy and will be deceived by the prophesied strong delusion which God will send upon those who do not love the truth and who delight in wickedness.

Those who are lukewarm and apostate should heed the warning of Revelation 3:14-19 —

To the angel of the church in Laodicea write: These are the words of the Amen, the faithful and true Witness, the Ruler of God's creation. I know your deeds, that you are neither cold nor hot. I wish you were either one or the other! So, because you are lukewarm — neither hot nor cold — I am about to spit you out of My mouth. You say, "I am rich; I have acquired wealth and do not need a thing." But you do not realize that you are wretched, pitiful, poor, blind and naked. I counsel you to buy from Me gold refined in the fire, so you can become rich; and white clothes to wear, so you can cover your shameful nakedness; and salve to put on your eyes, so you can see. Those whom I love I rebuke and discipline. So be earnest, and repent.

The second type I see being raised up throughout the world are committed believers totally sold out to Jesus Christ. These Biblical Christians are developing discipline and self-control in every aspect of their lives. They are refusing to be tainted by the wickedness in this world. They have a love for the truth and are diligently studying God's Word, praying, and fasting. They are seeking the Lord with all their hearts and have a hunger and desire for Him as never before. They are walking in the genuine power of His Spirit (not all the imitation and counterfeit), and will not conform for the temporary popularity and convenience of a unified apostate church. In spite of difficulty, opposition, and persecution, they refuse to compromise the Word of God and their testimony for Jesus. The Lord is using them in a tremendous way — giving them discernment, wisdom, courage, strength, and His anointing.

Stand Victoriously for the Lord

The choice is yours — apostate Christianity or Biblical Christianity. Which will you chose? Will you be lukewarm, fall by the wayside, become deceived and caught in the apostasy? Or will you be one who honestly says, "Lord, I want to serve You with all my heart!"

Do not be half-committed, compromising, and cowardly. Instead, be totally committed to Jesus Christ — then you will not only survive what is ahead, but empowered by His Spirit will be able to stand victoriously for the Lord.

Behold, I am coming soon! My reward is with Me, and I will give to everyone according to what he has done. ... He [Jesus] who testifies to these things says, "Yes, I am coming soon." Amen. Come, Lord Jesus.

— Revelation 22:12,20

FOR MORE INFORMATION:

Bill Rudge has produced numerous books, pamphlets, and cassettes on a variety of other timely topics. For a complete listing and a copy of his informative newsletter, write to:

Bill Rudge Ministries
P.O. Box 108
Sharon, PA 16146-0108